EIGHT INSIGHTFUL
UPANISHADS

1. Isha 2. Kena 3. Katha 4. Mandukya
5. Mundaka
6. Prashna 7. Aitareya 8. Shvetashvatara

Ashwini Kumar Aggarwal

ISBN13: 9789392201356 Paperback Edition
ISBN13: 9789392201400 Hardbound Edition
ISBN13: 9789392201417 Digital Edition

Title: **Eight Insightful Upanishads**
Author: **Ashwini Kumar Aggarwal**

Printed and Published by
Devotees of Sri Sri Ravi Shankar Ashram
34 Sunny Enclave, Devigarh Road
Patiala 147001, Punjab, India

https://advaita56.weebly.com/
The Art of Living Centre

https://www.artofliving.org/

24th July 2021, Guru Poornima, Sarvartha Siddhi Yoga
Shukla Paksha, Ashadha Masa, Varsha Ritu, Uttara Ashadha
Nakshatra, Simon Bolivar Day celebrated on 24th July by Venezuela,
Ecuador, Bolivia, Peru, Colombia.
Vikram Samvat 2078 Ananda, Saka Era 1943 Plava

1st Edition July 2021

जय गुरुदेव

Sri Sri Ravi Shankar

who loves us and makes our world charming

Blessing

All that you can do is to raise the level of Sattva. And then when Sattva's level is high, we have to wait one moment, any moment knowledge can dawn there.

All that you can do to have sunlight in this room, is to open the curtains and keep the windows open. And when dawn comes, it just dawns. You have the sunlight inside.

Sri Sri Ravi Shankar
A discourse on Yogasara Upanishad

Acknowledgements

Guru Poornima Guru Puja Havan Meditation and Sudarshan Kriya.

Cover Photo Credits

Amroz playing the Grand Piano on her birthday, the 8th of September, a rendering of "The Entertainer" by Scott Joplin.

Preface

In an Advanced Meditation Course, Mind stops.
Consciousness heals. Body knows no complaint.
Heart feels nice and warm. Lord walks in.

Veda	
Mantra Verses (Samhita)	Brahmana Verses
	Brahmana Aranyaka Upanishad

Adi Shankaracharya's masterly commentary on eleven
Upanishads is the de facto standard for Vedanta. These
eleven have been named the principal Upanishads. Though
it is said there are 1180 Upanishads written over a period of
a thousand years, actual manuscripts available as of now
are 108 only.

A chart that lists the eleven Upanishads commented on in detail by Sankara.

Rigveda	Samaveda	<u>Shukla Yajurveda</u> Krishna Yajurveda	Atharvaveda
Gives the fundamental laws of creation	Gives the intrinsic harmony within creation	Gives the specific design, administrative and governing principles for a family or a nation	Gives the specific ritucharya and dinacharya for an individual
Aitareya	Kena **Chandogya**	Ishavasya **<u>Brihadaranyaka</u>** Katha Taittiriya Shvetashvatara	**Mandukya** Mundaka Prashna
प्रज्ञानम् ब्रह्म	तत् त्वम् असि	अहं ब्रह्म अस्मि	अयम् आत्मा ब्रह्म

Four great illuminating statements or mahavakyas are listed above with their corresponding Upanishads in **bold**.

Vedic Sanskrit can never be adequately translated. It has sutras and dictums that can each form an entire school curriculum. The only way is to wait until words and sentences sprout after deep meditation in the presence of an enlightened master.

Table of Contents

Qualifications Prerequisites

The Upanishad is a masterly text, meant for a sincere and serious aspirant. Basic qualifications include a command over language and neatness in attire.

Prerequisites most needed to imbibe the knowledge are:
- Respectfulness
- Readiness to serve with cheerfulness
- Discipline for a year with frugal lifestyle
- Truthfulness and candor in communication

1 The Isha Upanishad

All Upanishads begin with a Prayer. A prayer is simply being silent for a moment, collecting one's thoughts and awareness, withdrawing it from the external. Only then the inner light can shine through.

Shanti Mantra

oṃ pūrṇamadaḥ pūrṇamidaṃ pūrṇāt pūrṇamudacyate ।
pūrṇasya pūrṇamādāya pūrṇamevāvaśiṣyate ॥
oṃ śāntiś śāntiś śāntiḥ ॥

This SHANTI MANTRA is an invocation that is recited before the Isha and other Upanishads of the Shukla Yajurveda.

Meaning

From the infinity a fullness is born. That is again amply infinite. When this supreme contentment showers bliss, all who receive become filled with love, everyone's heart overflows. It never diminishes.

Peace in the Environs. Peace in the Mind-Body-Being. Peace in the Soul.

Ishavasya Upanishad constitutes the final chapter (4oth adhyāya) of the Shukla Yajurveda from verse 1959 onwards, and survives in two recensions, named Kanva Shakha and Madhyandina Shakha. Its verses are written in Anushtup meter, i.e., having 32 syllables each. A single statement consists of 16 syllables, just like the Bhagavad Gita.

Goes by various names, i.e. Ishavasya Upanishad, Isha Upanishad, Ishavasyopanishad, Ishopanishad.

1. An all-powerful supreme divinity permeates and envelops this – creation - composed of the active and passive, matter and energy, living and non-living.

Realizing this sacred *separateness*, having unswerving faith in its indestructibility, live life to the full.

How may life be lived to the maximum potential? Simply by following the discipline of non-covetousness, or non-injury.

Refer the striking similarity of this verse from the 8th canto of Srimad Bhagavatam Mahapurana.

2. Life is meaningful and divine, be a karma yogi, do honest hard work.

Dream big giving full reign to your aspirations; plan to live many fruitful productive years.

Thus by not giving up, by participating fully and giving 100% efforts in day to day life, you shall be free of guilt, regret, fear or blame.

---

3. Chaotic, cluttered, binding and frustrating becomes your world when you shun discipline.

When you live without a proper education, your intellect and senses get blinded by insanity.

Then you meander amongst barbaric brutes, inhuman and wasteful is your existence.

---

4. Understand well the nature of the illuminating self within. The Self is Stillness Harmony personified. The Self thinks and acts quicker than the brain.

The Self though *actionless and unmoving* reaches everywhere, obtains everything.

The Self is pure consciousness, an unattached witness.

Like a mother it sustains and supports, like air it infuses life.
It is due to its presence alone that all events happen and all
beings work and play.

---

5. The Self glides, yet moves not.
The Self is afar, yet right close.

All is filled with the pure consciousness; all is enveloped by it
fully.

This knowledge is the key. This oneness is to be realized. It is
to be strongly ingrained in one's fiber; it should be at the
back of one's mind when dealing with the wealthy or the
poor, with the saint or the prejudiced, with humans or with
four-legged, nay even with life or non-life.

---

6. The Saint sees this Oneness. The Seer experiences this
within. So does any who is devoted to his duty.

And what do you get out of this attitude?
Unbelievable clarity and focus and determination.

And how come?

Simple. Mind is without fear. There is no bitterness in the consciousness. There isn't any enmity. You are not draining your energies in trying to conceal anything. When you do not have an antagonist, your progress is turbo charged, brimming with successes.

7. When people experience such a divinity in any form, it also brushes off on them.

Grace takes firm hold of the seeker, the aspirant becomes aware; his faculties, senses and intellect become soaked in the purity.

There is no infatuation then. There is no sorrow there. The oneness becomes firmly rooted, the heart has attained steadfastness.

8. Such a person established in the Self, in who trust and faith and contentment have matured, hear about him.

He shines and glows, his body encounters no opposition from man or nature, his mind is unbiased, no arrows or barbs get thrown at him. He radiates the truth and is above all blame.

The intelligent soul has nature and elements at his command or is in complete harmony with nature. He is whom the lord has chosen, on him grace has fallen.

He lives the Truth, he knows the Reality, he is the essence of creation. Open as space, people sense freedom in his presence. Untarnished by time his value system, his teachings span eons.

9. Folk who disregard education, culture or norms of society are gripped by a great insecurity and live in utter depravation.

The intelligent who become perverted, who use their cleverness or skills to wreck destruction; their lot is even worse. Their soul knows no peace.

10. Many and varied are the results gotten by those who practice discipline and do their duty sensibly.

Similarly, those who lead an undisciplined and wanton existence, their lives also teach us many things.

Sometimes the logic may neither be easily explainable nor be palatable; the overall results and effects of actions may not be seen in one lifetime.

Such is the wisdom heard from the mouths of the brave.

Who have elucidated and distilled the truth for our benefit. Who have lived patiently without jumping to conclusions. Who have always given a fair chance and the benefit of doubt to the opposition.

---

11. Practice self-discipline and live responsibly. Learn from the mistakes of others and do not fall into the same ditch.

Both success and failure are great teachers, each failure is a stepping stone to success.

Overcome challenges by proper education and seeking good counsel.

Planning for the worst and investing in sound design helps in the long run and misery is prevented or overcome.

12. Living a life of arrogance, divide-n-rule, polarization and extreme ambition is a blueprint for disaster.

On the other hand, just being goody goody, not applying commonsense; trying to run away from the world; having a one-track mind; thinking that one is very religious and being overtly righteous, doing spiritual acts merely as a ritual; any of this is a sure recipe for tarnishing the soul and becoming shrouded in foggy frustrations.

13. Aiming for the highest is not the same as aiming for the pleasurable; this has been the constant refrain through the ages.

Determine with a sound conscience, whether petty comfort is your goal or whether it is some noble thought that is fraught with many challenges and demands sustained spirited effort.

Such a life of honour has been lived by the brave, such is the example set that has inspired millions over the globe.

14. The brave is inspired by the great deeds, and he also acknowledges the frailties in the world. He takes both in his stride.

He makes it a point to learn from peoples and events, and lives with awareness without turning a blind eye or despising the wicked.

Thus is victory gained, thus is immortality achieved, thus does his life become a shining beacon for many.

---

15. The Truth is covered by a golden veil. Plainness hides profound wisdom. Calm waters run deep. A saint cannot be known by his skin.

O Lord! Please part the flimsy covering from your face, so that I may behold your loveliness.

May I get the divine vision, see the path I should tread. Know when to act and when to let go.

---

16. O Bliss giver! O Solitude lover!
O Discipline enforcer! O Energizer of all! O Creator!
O multi-talented multi-skilled Brilliance!

Please allow me to approach, please reduce your glare. So

that your beauty I may adore. So that your absolute goodness I may gain.

Grant that I may unite with thee, merge into thyself and become One.

May I express and live the Divinity. THAT I AM.

---

17. The gale is whipping me towards thee. My stains are wiped away, faults reduced to ashes.

Om! May i remember the noble deeds, may I not forget the sacred promises.

---

18. O Benevolent Fire!

May we digest and assimilate the wisdom, (just as thee cook our meals and give us our daily strength).

May we grow by performing meritorious deeds and enjoy the fruits of our toils.

O Knower of our weaknesses, show us how to overcome them; and Knower of our strengths, may we not get waylaid by them.

Our obeisance to thee again and again.

Praises shower on thee, humility and gratefulness fill the heart.

(The same mantra is in Rig Veda 1.189.01)

‖ iti īśopaniṣat ‖ END.

2 The Kena Upanishad

Shanti Mantra

oṃ āpyāyantu mamāṅgāni vākprāṇaścakṣuḥ śrotramatho

balamindriyāṇi ca sarvāṇi | sarvaṃ brahmaupaniṣadam ,

māhaṃ brahma nirākuryāṃ , mā mā brahma nirākarod ,

anirākaraṇam astu anirākaraṇaṃ me'stu | tadātmani nirate

ya upaniṣatsu dharmāste mayi santu te mayi santu ||

oṃ śāntiḥ śāntiḥ śāntiḥ ||

Peace Invocation

O Divine Wisdom!
May all my limbs function well together.
May my speech and eyes and ears perform above par and
my breath be deep and steady.
I have heard all is Brahman, may this Upanishad filter down
to my cells and bones, fiber and sinews.
May good sense and the right vision not elude me.
May the great Lord be by my side and not forsake me when I
disrespect or disregard Him.
May I really feel His presence and get His feedback from time
to time.
May I be fully qualified to receive the Upanishad.
May my intellect receive it with open arms and a Yes mind.
Peace in our heart, in our body and in our environs.

Kena is from the Sama Veda. It elucidates the deepest quest
of the awakened being, the soul-searching Questions…

- WHAT is it that impels me?
- WHY is it that I do what I do?
- HOW come I succeed, and at times fail?
- Is there a Template or Blueprint?

Kena Upanishad gets its name from the starting word of its first verse, viz. *kena iṣitaṃ patati preṣitaṃ manaḥ* ׀ By WHAT inspired does my intellect function?
"kena" =Instrumental singular case 3/1 of neuter stem "kim".

Kenopanishad is also called Jaimini Brahmana or Talavakara Brahmana, by the name of the Rishi to whom it is attributed.

atha Kena Upaniṣad (*kenopaniṣad*)

Now begins the Kena Upaniṣad

Upaniṣad means a deep connection with the Master. The inward journey begins when one sits still.

A profound question arises. If all is willed by the Divine, what is good and what is evil? On the absolute plane it is all ONE. On the transactional plane myriad names and forms arise. There is an interplay of the natural forces and energies. The energies are simply playing, a leela, however as mortals we experience joy or grief. Just a shade of emotion; not absolute; only a different color, and we give them epithets of good, ugly, attractive, painful.

The question arises, can the painful be avoided? Can the good be enhanced? The Master teaches that for someone who follows the principles enunciated in the Veda, there is a steady enhancement of the good and the pain recedes finally. Not that the harsh and cruel events stop arising. But one's tolerance, alertness, and fitness have risen sufficiently so as not to be easily awed or put down by them.

But what is my will and what is the Divine will? Are they really two? As if two. As a mirage. As the rising and setting of the sun. All the backdrop of a grand spectacle.

Chapter 1

So we can experience the full range of emotions. So one can have various experiences. Play many games to avoid boredom. Difficult to answer, perhaps the answer is not in words. Daresay just my relative opinion.

Yes but what is my will and what is the divine will?

Anything that leads one to Joy. To lasting Joy. Peace. That can be termed as the divine will. And the play is so designed such that this path seems fraught with thistles and thorns. Known as the Shreyas, the path towards liberation.

The other one designed to offer quick pleasure is the Preyas. We can just spend many years in the wilderness, hankering for small sensual trophies.

For the Divine, it does not matter. For the Individual it definitely matters. One can spend life cheerfully or one can live in doubt, suspicion, and despair. The choice is mine. Both roles are available. Both roles are needed. Advaita to Dvaita to Advaita, the wheel comes full circle.

I seek Counsel, Help, or make a Start

1.1 O Beloved Master!
By whose inspiration does my intellect reason? Who doth direct my speech so? What power controls my sight and hearing?

I know very well the iPhone has been designed by Steve Jobs, the internet we all use is Tim Berners-Lee's gift to mankind, my home is the blueprint of architect Jiwan Gupta. And I am writing this book.

But who or what is that makes my body and being function? Who rules my breath? Who gives me the thoughts? Who colors my moods and makes the emotions arise within? Who rules all that goes on within me and what makes the brain tick?

By What (Whom) impelled, nay specially inspired is the intellect drawn to?
By What yoked to is the first breath taken?
By What impelled is this speech, do they say?
The eye, the ear; indeed what power yokes (to make them functional)?

1.2 My dear Child! THAT which is the director of the ears and controller of the mind. Indeed that ONE is also governing the speech and making the breath move. And verily looking through the eyes.

Upon close scrutiny of THAT, the brave learn to cope up exceedingly well in this life. And those committed to the Truth never ever grieve.

Indeed THAT is the hearing ability of the ear, reasoning ability of the intellect, speaking skill of the speech, breathing apparatus of the breath, vision of the eye.

Only after having fully freed, having gotten over (all temptations or indiscipline) from this world; the brave ones attain liberation (from misery).

1.3 To THAT subtle controlling plane, sight does not reach. Nor do words. Nor does the intellect of any man.

THAT is an unknown domain. Even none knows how to describe it or comprehend it or talk about it.

THAT is beyond knowledge. THAT is beyond reason. Since we have no words, we can say THAT is neither knowable, nor can THAT be said to be unknowable.

Such is the sum total of all experience from time immemorial. Such has been the understanding of our ancestors, the elders and the learned.

In a nutshell, neither anything conclusive nor definite regarding THAT has ever been declared.

There sight reaches not,
speech does not make sound,
not even the intellect (fathoms).
Hence we do not know by what method IT could be discussed.
THAT is quite different from the measurable,
from the immeasurable also IT is quite unlike.
Thus we have heard from our ancestors,
who explained THAT to us.

1.4 THAT which words cannot express, yet all that gets expressed through words; THAT has been called The

Brahman.

Know that Brahman to be the Absolute Reality.

With great courage, understand,
what goes about in this transactional world is only the
apparent reality.

WHAT by the word cannot be told,
By WHAT the word gets generated.
THAT as "the Brahman" you must understand,
IT is not this (deities and statues and various forms) which men
worship.

Mankind has evolved various names and forms for His worship.
There are many representations of God's form. The Great Lord
has been depicted in so many colors with a range of attributes,
skills, and emotions, and called by as many names. All of that is
fine. This verse simply adds and says, God is much more than
that. God is not only that since we cannot fully encapsulate
Him in the limited frame of a Body-Mind complex.

1.5 THAT which needs no mind to think, in fact THAT
whose creation is the mind; know THAT Brahman to be the
ultimate worth seeking for.

Do not be waylaid by the aims and aspirations of petty men.

THAT which cannot be comprehended by the intellect,
Rather, due to WHAT the intellect functions, the wise have so
declared.

Much much Bigger than anyone's definition is the great Lord.

A whole lot different than your perception or experience is He.

1.6 THAT which needs no eye to see, THAT whose creation is the eye; know THAT Brahman to be the all-Seeing Eye.

Do not be duped by doctors who imagine they can fix eyesight.

THAT which by the eye is not discernible,
By WHAT all eyes see.
He is beyond definition, He cannot be described, His nature does not fit in any school book or rule book. Laws cannot bind Him. The WORD cannot describe Him.

1.7 THAT which needs no ear to hear, THAT whose creation is the ear; know THAT Brahman to be the ultimate sound source.

Be sure that the singer or the musician is simply a window to the sounds emanating from Brahman.

THAT which one does not hear by the ear,
By WHAT the ear hears any sound.
All the world's stories, and all of mankind's exploits and experiences fall short of expressing the Lord's character.

1.8 THAT which doesn't need to breathe, THAT whose creation is the breath; know THAT Brahman to be the breath of this world's beings.

Get to know the reality that whatever moves and flows and seems alive and well, is simply a movie projected by the Brahman.

The One who gives life to all, the one who makes all involuntary functions to happen, the Creator of the black-holes, galaxies, gravitational, electric, magnetic, and light energies; know all that to be just a tiny reflection of the actual Thing.

THAT which breathes not by the breath,
By WHAT the breath does get breathed.

‖ iti prathamaḥ khaṇḍaḥ ‖
Here ends the first chapter.

For some of us this much teaching is good enough to get well-settled in life. For other disciples more education is needed, so the next part.

Chapter 2

Our life may be symbolized by a Rubik's cube. It has 3 layers.

Some of us can keep our first layer – the body – very attractive looking. We are good at solving one side of the puzzle quickly.

Many are very good citizens in society, keeping both their body and mind stable, clear, and functional.

The rare one is able to solve all three layers with élan, keeping body and mind fit, heart free of blemish, and <u>Aim towards the SUPREME.</u>

The Guru or Master is such a divine presence. He or she epitomizes the Lord, accessible to all humans who seek liberation. The Master teaches – "Now you have had enough of this world. Now refocus, realign, make the leap inwards, aim towards the very core of your being. Keeping all aside, light the LAMP within".

THAT, Brahman, The Good Lord, Guru

For many years it remains blurred. Inconspicuous. Unknown. Not needed. There is enough to do. There are many sights and sounds, the world is already moving in a certain way. Peer pressures are high, the news and media have gotten all entangled to _their_ point of view. Big, Bigger, Biggest. For each the definition is different, yet it is actually the same. Wealth, Power, Fame hog the limelight. Names change, places vary, victories remain confined to sensual achievements. Quick Quicker Quickest. Yes we made it before anyone, but where to?

The Brahman has an intense liking for the ones who reach the top in any field. THAT Presence then ITSELF descends to enlighten the entrepreneurs. THAT Being alone changes the direction of the brightest. Not on the physical plane. On the reasoning plane. On the plane of the citta. Our memories, experiences, conclusions get redrawn, re-inked, reassessed. The physical events remain the same. Only the importance we attach to them has changed. Our vision wakes up and rises forth from its limited bodyMind concepts. We can then embrace the infinity. We can then accept, acknowledge and willingly make friends with the UNKNOWN.

2.1 Whoever howsoever learned and well read and experienced they might be, if they proclaim that they know the Brahman; consider it truly they know little if at all!

THAT which gives you life and meaning, THAT which causes the energies and natural laws in creation, ponder on THAT. THAT alone is relevant and worth directing your efforts and aims for.

How much does anyone really know? Is the functioning of the brain known? Is there much control over the thoughts? Emotions? Feelings?

Can you really tell when someone will be born or someone will pass away?

Do you really think the mysteries of the great oceans have been resolved? What about deep Space, intelligent life elsewhere and the size, structure, shape and composition of our universe?

If you think IT is well known, thus;
Scarce indeed you know of Brahman's nature.
THAT of which you are,
THAT of which the superior beings are;
Now surely one must just ponder deeply,
(The findings of) the wise alone need to be well thought over,
in my opinion.

The Master goes on to teach

2.2 I do not believe i know THAT, yet i cannot truthfully say i have no knowledge of THAT either.

Those whom the world calls Enlightened, of those Saintly
ones we cannot fathom the extent of their wisdom, strength
or prowess.

<u>A Beauty of a statement. A Masterly statement. Like a Maha
Vayka that transcends SPACETIME. Leaves the panca
mahabhutas behind. Overcomes the three gunas.</u>

I do not think IT is well grasped by me,
Nor indeed entirely unknown to me can thus be said.
Those who consider IT not fully understood by them are the
ones who know IT is not unknown to them.

*This is a Maha Vakya, a Great Statement or Law. Only the
humble student goes far. Only the one who is sincerely seeking
reaches anywhere. Here the essential trait of a disciple has
been stated. This statement underlines the premise for any
invention, discovery or attainment.*

2.3 Those who do their duties fluently are the ones in
whom Brahman works the best.

Those who idle away their lives or are known to cause harm
have Brahman operating quite dimly within them.

**The one who does not lay claim over IT has ownership of IT,
The one who claims IT, he has no inkling of IT.
Stupid are those who bluster or brag knowledge,
Wise are those who prefer discretion.**

*More guidelines for the budding student. Character building
and humility ingraining go together.*

2.4 Wherever one sees confidence, clarity and sound

vision, know it to be Brahman's fluid working.

Those brave souls who live by their guts have Brahman operating the best.

Those saintly beings whose wisdom spreads far and wide, know them to have been granted immortality in Time and Space by Brahman.

Awakened-knowledge is verily supposed to manifest enlightenment.
By his guts the brave succeeds,
By learning, enlightenment he obtains.

Alertness, Awareness, Self-reliance, Earnest and Sincere seeking are the traits for Success.

2.5 Here and now if one becomes united with this wisdom; consider it one has attained life's quest, one has fulfilled all responsibility.

Till such time of attainment of Yoga, keep on striving hard, lest you regret.

The Saint sees Brahman's hand in all happenings everywhere. Thus the wise are revered and remembered by countless across eons.

Surely who realizes here itself, attains the imperishable truth.
The one who forgoes efforts to realize, comes to great harm.
In the living, in the non-living, the undaunted discriminate,
From this world-web having transcended, they attain immortality.

|| iti dvitīyaḥ khaṇḍaḥ ||
Here ends the second part of the teaching.

Chapter 3

The Guru epitomizes love. Love of a rare kind. Love sans conflict, sans boundary, sans definition.

The Master's teaching filters deep down to every cell. It undoes coloring to the DNA. The calm unhurried aura is what the heart longs for. Profound peace, solidified silence, and ready action infuses nectar into the far corners of every nucleus. A joy wells up. One feels whole, well, taken care of, and empowered to shoulder responsibility.

The Guru speaks from a space of spotless liquid love - *niranjana*. His words are not polarized in any way.

Talents blossom. Projects get done. The stage comes alive with happiness, laughter peals, and enthusiastic yells.

All roles get applauded, none is the minor, the spotlight escapes no one.

The Folly of the Righteous or the stumbling block for the Great

Now comes the story time. The best orator, the acclaimed speaker, the famous school is the one that gives due attention to anecdote, entertainment, live examples, practical wisdom.

The Master superbly weaves a story, that is actually a FACT of common occurrence in daily life. So many high performers and great artists get laurels. Many thinkers and scientists are granted the Nobel prize or the Padma

Bhushan award. The daily newspapers are replete with many such events. Countless descriptions are given of the greatness, ingenuity, talent, hard work and faith of individuals.

The Master carefully outlines an incident of great victory, and makes the protagonists ponder. Is there any higher intelligence? Is there someone apart from us who is running the whole show?

Best are those who acknowledge the Lord willingly. The Best of the Best is the one who sees the Lord's hand early on.

|| atha tṛtīyaḥ khaṇḍaḥ ||

Now the third part of the teaching.
(Illustration, Allegory, Story).

3.1 By Brahman's doing the great men acquired fame and fortune. By Brahman's will they ascended to great heights and dominated the world.

Some welled up in pride and thought - We are the greatest. We can beat anybody. We can overcome all odds. We can do anything.

Brahman indeed caused victory for the high officials.
In the victory brought about by Brahman,
verily the high officials became exalted.
This victory is solely our doing they thought,
"This greatness is ours alone", thus.

3.2 The Brahman sensed their vain pride. To banish their stupidity a play was enacted. Those puffed-up souls had no inkling of what was to unfold.

A large glow appeared, it made the palatial glitter of the great parliament pale and dim in comparison.

In the Indian tradition, the Devas are supposed to be light beings, or energies that have very little matter content. Energy as in Fire energy, Wind energy, etc. So when Brahman wishes to make them realize their folly, IT deputes a Yakṣa – a large light – a huge glow - an energy much bigger than them – to their vicinity.

Verily IT of (such thoughts) sensed,
For them (to notice their folly) a great light IT manifested,
Who this Great Orb, this they(high officials) knew not.

A masterly telling, where the Lord himself comes to the rescue by creating an event for one to realize, and thereby maintain the glory and nobility for a longer length of time.

In the "locker room"-"back stage"-"many unnamed persons and events" who are equally responsible in our success are to be given due credit. Notice Guruji's favorite mantra before eating *"annadātā sukhī bhava.* May the farmer who grows the grain, the merchant who sells, and the mother who cooks; be well taken care of." By this, the food shall nourish me better and aid in my success.

3.3 The world's council chose their eldest and brightest candidate to investigate the matter. He was named Agni the Fierce.

They spoke to Agni,
"O Knower of all Existence! This (fact) you find out who is this Yakṣa?" ,
"So be it", thus (Agni replied).

3.4 Agni flew towards the bright orb.

He heard the question - "Who approaches"? Cheekily he answered - "I am Agni the all-consumer and all-knower".

Towards the (glowing orb) he (Agni) advanced aggressively.
To him, the Glow respectfully addressed, "Who art thee?"
"Truly I am the Fire", thus he replied,
"truly I am the Knower of all Creation", thus.

3.5 To which came the calm reply, "Really? Are you really capable of anything"?

Agni danced and leapt high, replied flippantly, "Certainly I can devour the entire world, apart from lighting it up thoroughly".

In you what is then the greatest specialty? (asked the Yakṣa of Agni).
This all I could reduce to ashes.
Also, on this earth whatever (exists).

3.6 Brahman's bright orb coolly set forth a blade of grass and said, "Could you please devour this tiny morsel"?

Agni tried with all his might, his many flames leaping in all directions, yet that blade of grass remained unruffled and unscathed.

Facing utter defeat, Agni returned humbled and accepted his incompetence in investigating the matter.

For him a blade of grass was set (by the Yakṣa),
"This can you burn?" (asked the Yakṣa).
With full speed towards it Agni rushed,
that to burn he was not able,
he from there instantly retreated,
THIS to discern he was not able,
knew not what this Yakṣa.

3.7 The world's council then picked Vayu, their fastest and most dynamic officer. He was sent forth to unravel the case.

Now they spoke to Vayu,
"O Wind! This (fact) you find out who is this Yakṣa?",
So be it, thus (Vayu replied).

3.8 Vayu reached the bright orb instantly.

He heard the question, "Who goes"? Impudently he answered, "I am Vayu that gives life as a mother to all that moves".

Towards the (glowing orb) he (Vayu) advanced haughtily.
To him, the Glow respectfully addressed, "Who art thee"?
Truly I am the Wind, thus he replied,
truly I am the the Mother that breathes life in all of Creation,
thus.

3.9 To which came the calm reply, "Wonderful! So you can actually make something move"?

"What do you mean?" asked Vayu the Wind belligerently. "I can blow away the entire world in a puff".

In you what is then the greatest specialty? (asked the Yakṣa of Vayu).
This all I could blow away.
Also, on this earth whatever (exists).

3.10 Brahman's Yaksha (a powerful messenger) presented him with a blade of grass and said - Could you please give this some air and movement?

Vayu huffed and puffed to no avail. The solitary twig remained unmoved as if it was in vacuum.

Meekly the Wind accepted his downfall and returned a better person.

For him a blade of grass was set (by the Yakṣa),
"This can you blow away?" (asked the Yakṣa).
With full speed towards it Vayu rushed,
that to blow away he was not able,
he from there hastily turned back,
THIS to discern he was unable,
understood not what this Yakṣa was upto.

The word "hasty retreat" is used in the sense of acceptance of defeat, rather than in the sense of harboring resentment.

3.11 Finally running out of ideas, the council deputed their president Indra to get at the root of the matter.

Even before the president could make his move, it became quite dark and the bright halo was nowhere to be seen.

Now they spoke to Indra,
"O Lord of Senses! This (fact) you find out who is this Yakṣa?",
So be it thus (Indra replied),
towards THAT he swiftly advanced,
but IT vanished from sight (before Indra could reach).

3.12 A fair maiden made its appearance with skin like the softest, purest, fresh snowfall.

To this most beautiful divine presence, the president asked in all humility - Kindly enlighten me to what's going on? I thought i knew everything and had all the powers. Yet this is beyond me and even my best and brightest men have failed in this regard.

Beauty is called forth to dazzle the senses. She has the greatest chance of delighting the stubbornest candidate. Not only does great Beauty win over the intellect and pacify the memory, she also makes one see the point clearly.

Diplomacy is the key in today's world. Diplomacy was the triumph then.

Dialogue helps resolve many issues, for dialog to succeed, a welcoming and graceful atmosphere needs to be created.

In that common space he came upon a lady of unparalleled beauty,
To her, Uma the Snow-maiden, he asked;
"Who is this Yaksa", what is its mission?

Here ends the third part of the Upanishad.

The illustration ends. The student can either grasp the essence here itself and be done with the learning, or he might want further education.

Chapter 4

Divine Mother corrects the Vision and the Master gives the Keys to Emancipation

The final part of the teaching commences. All points are fluidly laid out.

Finally the disciple is asked to pursue
- Cheerfulness,
- Discipline,
- Honest Hard Work,
- Seeking proper guidance in critical aspects, and
- Sincerity

to succeed in life.

4.1 The benevolent Mother then in a tone of gentle rebuke said that there was no need to get into doership.

Any victory and every success was primarily due to grace and credit was due to the Supreme Lord.

By this teaching the president realized his folly and atoned for it with good cheer.

The Brahman, thus she answered.
From Brahman's hand indeed in the victory have you all grown exalted.
At that moment he realized the Brahman.

In her glance and that word, enlightenment happened.

When P.V. Sindhu wins the badminton world championship, who has been primarily instrumental? When I land the perfect job as Professor at Sri Sri University, whom does the credit go to? How come the idea of inventing a light bulb came to Edison or that of an ac-motor to Tesla? What is the reason than Google or Apple have reached the zenith and so many others are struggling to even make both ends meet?

In a very subtle, almost easy to miss, and practically forgotten manner; the Master; who is himself Brahman personified, clothes himself behind this allegory. He lays the clear foundation for the intrinsic cause for all greatness in this world. He lays the onus of Doership on Brahman. If we study closely the greatest of the great souls - Socrates, Lao Tzu, Florence Nightingale, Adi Shankaracharya, Albert Einstein - we shall notice their works akin to that of an invisible energy moving through them.

4.2 So it has been said, the rulers of nations are appointed by the Lord Himself. They who become emperors have the backing of Brahman. It is through the best and brightest in every land that Brahman's presence is clearly perceived.

That is how the natural forces in creation, Gravitation Indra, Light Agni and Air Vayu came to have universal appeal. These powers had the closest experience of Brahman's working.

As indeed they (physically and mentally) to IT came the closest,
Therefore truly Agni, Vayu, Indra, these (three) luminaries are as if ranked above all the other officials.
They certainly were the first to realize the Brahman.

Honor is given to the first in any venture. Honorable are they who achieve the goal before others and show the path to succeeding generations.

In the Indian tradition, the natural forces and energies have always been considered **intelligent-thinking-planning-executing entities**, *albeit with a much bigger domain than mere mortals. The gravitational force (Indra), the atmosphere (Vayu), and the light energy (Agni), have always been depicted as superior human beings. This adds a human-like mysterious, emotional, and unpredictable behaviour to them. This enhances their interpretation and is a much better definition than classifying them to be mere physical forces of nature.*

4.3 Gravitation Indra is all pervasive in the galaxies, black holes and stellar dust; since it was the First who acknowledged the Lord and His divine presence.

Indra verily came the nearest to Its touch,
Hence he is considered the best amongst the other forces.
He certainly was the first to realize the Brahman.

He was the earliest adventurer to accept the presence of the Lord with firm conviction.

<u>grammar note:</u>
In English, we consider the gravitation force as a natural energy and give it the neuter gender, while in Sanskrit it is infused with life *Indra* and given the masculine gender.

On the other hand the all-pervasive Lord Brahman has been said to be formless or having all attributes simultaneously, so Sanskrit gives it the neuter gender.

The use of *pluta vowel* "आ३" is seen in the Upanishads. Listening to the chanting makes the body resound with uncommon happiness. When the diva or soprano takes a note to the high and holds it there, that is the ultimate crowning moment.

4.4 All of us also have sensed and had the good fortune of seeing the mighty Lord's work, in a manner of speaking.

Whether in the flash of lightning or the drooping of an eyelid. Or even in the beautiful glance from someone that restores our balance, peace, and enthusiasm.

Commoners sense a divine hand only in the miraculous. In something that they cannot reproduce or control. Brave are the heroes who offer every little moment to His benevolence.

Such is its demonstration,
Like in the lightening that flashed momentarily,
Also the Lord is undoubtedly sensed in the twinkling of an eyelid.

4.5 So too in the Spiritual quest that surges forth in the devout seeker's heart. And in the intellect that goes forth in the passionate search for the ultimate truth.

Then

- one's being radiates with that purity of intent
- one's thoughts are directed laser like to THAT supreme aim.

Now summing up the essence;
And when the mind glimpses IT,
Then the germ of a thought manifests,
By that THIS is continuously remembered. (again and again refreshed and recalled in various events in one's life).

When the Grace falls upon a soul, something opens up within. A lamp is lit that illumines within. IT becomes the harbinger of Peace Prosperity Joy.

Shanti rastu, Pushti rastu, Tushti rastu.
Wish you Peace, Prosperity and Happiness.

4.6 Verily THAT is the most delightful aim that gladdens and nourishes the heart.

O Sincere One! Seek out with one-pointed attention THAT blissful Brahman.

The wise who senses the hand of the blissful Brahman in the entire phenomena verily notices a profound secret - all beings yearn for THAT and all forces only exemplify and exhibit THAT. Living like this the Saint becomes one with

Brahman. Then a day comes when the common folk and the high and mighty all seek the Saint.

THAT truly is named the BLISS,
That BLISS is worshipful,
The one who indeed knows THIS,

All beings seek-with-adoration, him.

The Saint is sought for by everyone since he knows with certainty that the Lord alone is worshipful.

Whereas we the commoners sense the Lord's hand only in rare moments or miracles, the saint sees the Lord's doing in every moment and every breath. The saint feels grateful for the good time, and is not ungrateful during the lean time. He acknowledges the infinite nature of the Lord, and himself lives the infinity. He keeps his calm even in the most trying situations, living in awe of the grand presence and its working.

The Master sums up

4.7 O devoted one! Thee had asked me of the WHO, of the WHAT that impels everything.

This sitting close of ours has become an Upanishad. Our wavelengths have matched, you have caught on between the lines, and the abstruse Truth has guided us all along.

Indeed we have sensed the unknowable, the Brahman has been with us throughout.

This is the accumulated wisdom of the entire lineage of holy saints and wise men who have walked this earth.

You requested for the Upanishad,
For you the intimate teaching was recited,
Of THAT Eternal indeed is the Upanishad that has been spoken by us.

the Master is invoking the lineage of enlightened saints while giving the discourse. This teaching is not an arbitrary imaginative discussion or opinion of a single person. It is the accumulated wisdom of mankind, the summum bonum of all cultures and races on our planet.

4.8 Earnestness in our spiritual quest, Restraint over our senses, and wholehearted efforts are the prerequisites in this venture.

Proper education, correct upbringing and presence of the Master is the essential toolkit. Truth that does not cause harm is the sheltering environment.

Tapas = Being cheerful. Taking the ups and downs in life in your stride. Accepting the harsh, tough, and dangerous moments without becoming bitter.

Damah = Following a standard. Having a value system and an ethical outlook. Incorporating discipline in life. Discipline in work, sleep, food habits, and entertainment.

Karma = Giving 100%. Living life to the fullest. Stretching yourself beyond the comfort zone. Expressing your talents and skills for common benefit. Nothing beats hard work.

Vedas = Collective wisdom. Good schooling. Broad vision.
Holistic and spiritual education.

Satyam = Truthfulness that does not cause hurt. Truth that
transcends conflict. Inner truth.

For attainment of THAT; austerity, discipline, and hard work
are the essential means,
The universal core teachings epitomize ITS glory and
attributes,
Sincerity is ITS very nature.

4.9 The one who conducts life in balance and is
committed to a holistic vision, from him grief-evil-hatred-
untruth drop away.

He finds everlasting peace, he attains to the blissful realms,
and his life becomes full and complete.

YES, such a life is worth living. Such a life alone counts in the
world of mankind.
The one who realizes THIS likewise,
having banished misfortune,
in the ultimate infinite heavenly plane resides.
Lives forever since he has transcended grief.

Here ends the Kena.
Thus ends this teaching on a note of promising lasting
HAPPINESS.

Isn't that what all ultimately seek?

3 The Katha Upanishad

Peace Invocation

oṃ saha nāvavatu | saha nau bhunaktu | saha vīryaṃ
karavāvahai | tejasvi nāvadhītamastu mā vidviṣāvahai ||
oṃ śānti śānti śāntiḥ ||

O Pure Loving Grace! May we be taken care of along with family and friends. May we enjoy socializing, eating, and outing together. May we support each other's vision and growth and May our intellect be open to new ideas and changing trends. May we spend more time in grateful praises, and May we discuss virtues rather than harp on vices. Peace in our heart, in our body, and in our environs.

Cast of Characters

1) Yama Mrityu. 2) Naciketa Gautama. 3) Vājaśravas.

- Yama = Mrityu, used to personify RESTRAINT, DEATH, TIME.
- Naciketa Gautama. Lineage or last name for Naciketa is Gautama. Thus used for Naciketa in Verses 2.1.15, 2.2.6, and for Vājaśravas in Verse 1.1.10.
- Vājaśravas

Vājaśravā is known for distributing in charity, *vāja* = food grains. His descendent gets named *vājaśravasaḥ* using Taddhita word derivation in Sanskrit Grammar. Also, another name given to the Rishi **Vājaśrava** is Aruna, the Sun's charioteer. By Sanskrit Grammar derivation rules, his

descendent can be named *āruṇiḥ* | Also *auddālakiḥ* the descendent of *uddālakaḥ*. Thus *auddālakiḥ* = *āruṇiḥ* = Vājaśravas, (see Verse 1.1.11) father of Naciketa in the story.

(Latin transliteration using IAST standard uses the spellings Yama, Naciketa, Vājaśravas. However normal English text will simply use the spellings Yama, Nachiketa, Vajashravas.)

Katha is mesmerizing to the core. It consists of imagery that has no parallel. It depicts the dialogue between the unlikeliest of protagonists - Yama and Nachiketa. Yama means Death. It also means King. Emperor. or very Old Man. Grandpa. or darkness stillness silence.
Simply put Yama means restraint. But of what kind? The restraint that cannot be tempted. The restraint that dares and flattens all temptations is Yama. And it also means Time or timeless. Aged or ageless.

What of Nachiketa? A young lad. A child of 8 or 9 years. One who has not even experienced teen. Yet one whose mind is crystal clear. Whose mind has not a ripple. Who can think through opacity. Who can navigate through dense fog. Who has a determination that cannot be deflected even an inch.

When i first heard Katha it was amazing. And when i listened to Guruji's discourse, especially Day Three tracks 10-11 BEYOND THE LAYERS OF EXISTENCE, it flashed like lightning in my brain.

Katha begins fabulously. When one has decided on the Ultimate goal, what does one do? Rarely in life does anyone go for the Highest. Is it so difficult? Yes.

How come? nor is it challenging only but it is also thankless. …in the beginning…that is why…almost thankless. the Best shall not Bless till the very last.
till each and every nerve and sinew,
each thought .word.deed fuses to aspire for that Alone.

(testimony. proof. all around you. Buddha. Socrates. Lao Tzu. Mahavir. Hanuman. Lincoln. Vinci. Einstein. Kabir GuruGobind. Jobs. Keller. Teresa. Christ. Lata. Musk. Sri Sri)

Kaṭha Upanishad is from the final eight sections of Krishna Yajurveda, from its Kaṭha recension, named after Kaṭha Rishi. Also called Kāṭhaka. Literally Kaṭha means story, so some spell it as Katha Upanishad. It consists of six sections in all, popularly visualized as two flowers each containing three petals that unfold as the aspirant imbibes and progresses.

Each petal has various veins. These are listed as 1.1.2 to indicate Flower.Petal.Vein = Chapter1.Topic1.Verse2, etc.

Flower 1 Petal 1

Characteristics of Nachiketa the Protagonist
or
The message of the Upanishad – what it behooves one to diligently practice

- Awareness-Alertness-Mindfulness
- Youthfulness
- Faith
- Contemplation-Meditation
- Patience-Endurance
- No Complaints
- Drop the Past
- Gratefulness
- Say No to Temptation
- Keep away from Greed
- Maintain Decorum

Once upon a time. desiring. Umm. of his.

Theme 1 The Great Duel

Such a magnificent beginning to Katha. Experience the profound depth of the plot.

1.1.1 Having decided on the Ultimate, the one-in-a-million householder embarks on the dangerous bleak road to Freedom. ..it is but certain that his most prized possession will be his biggest stumbling block…nay also his deliverance!

and the story unfolds to paint the picture of a man who gets down to square his things-thoughts-emotions and life.

his sole witness,
he himself in his childhood.

what is childhood? it is freedom. it is innocence. it is beauty. it is play. it does not know death. it is beyond fences.

what is adulthood? it is … not particularly envious. it is simply a euphemism for illness. slow death. or extended prison.

1.1.2 When i decide on a course of action, the best navigation comes from my own mind which was youthful some time back.

Only Health can opine fairly. Only Fitness can point the way to the brave. Only Youth that has not accumulated social dust can think clearly. From youth and fitness arises a supreme quality called FAITH that becomes the guiding principle.

Contemplation happens. I Meditate.

Indeed (as) charities distribution (was underway) Faith got hold
of him who was yet a young lad.
(Then) He pondered.

1.1.3 What am i up to? wonders my youth. Youth notices
blemishes straight away. i am being too careful. i am being
too straight forward. defensive that is sickening.

i have embarked on the brave. for sure dangers shall abound
in plenty. and here am i in dodge-adjust-fend mode???.

*Notice that Guruji delegates so much responsibility to the
youngsters in ashram. Almost all heads of departments and
secretaries are in their thirties or younger.*

**Passing on loans and debts, insults and weaknesses (in addition
to my strengths and wealth).
those joyless realms. namely.
he is deported to.**

1.1.4 Youth springs forth. Takes charge. Thunders thrice -
GO STRAIGHT FOR THE BEST. NO STOPPING. NO TURNING.

awakened i take the challenge with both arms wide - yes
certainly shall i meet Death on my own terms - unflinching -
calmly - unconcernedly - united within.

**Verily he asked his father, "O Blessed One! To whom shall I be
gifted?", thus. A second time, a third time.
Bluntly to him came the response,**

"To Death you shall proceed.", thus.

1.1.5 Certainly i am the pure. Without a doubt i am made of stuff that is a luxury in this creation.

What is it that i Finally WANT? Is there such a thing as an ending LIMIT?

The Upanishad is not at all talking about the physics. It knows that any wealth is earnable, any skill is learnable, any test is crackable and a girl is weddable.

The Upanishad knows that fears and guilts, hatreds and infatuations are much too slippery to admit to and vanquish. So it lays threadbare my weaknesses. Introducing the concept of "cow" it elucidates some key concepts -

cow = abundance and fundamental factor governing economy.
old cows = grandparents or senior citizens that we no longer can afford since their usefulness is gone.
milk = the only nourishment needed.
water = that is to be conserved or used wisely.

(7am 20th April. Annapurna Bhavan. Amrik Singh Road. By some good fortune i got invited to a food distribution morning. There was a motley group of poor or starving people including a couple and families who expectantly waited for a meal. As the serving started their faces lit up. Small children danced happily after taking a morsel. The couple's face broke into a wan smile. I hung my head in shame. Perhaps on other occasions i was them and they were me.)

Just an unknown event of no consequence that showed in

fine detail the fabric of creation. That is how Katha achieved legendary fame. By depicting starkly that the real protagonist was not the giver. That the receivers' presence made heroism possible. That youth was the key to transcend the TimeSpace puzzle.

That the Divine keeps the show going by enacting games and reversing roles. That beauty lies in the eyes of the beholder and not in the manifest.

1.1.6 Word is Law. The words uttered cannot be recalled. Words are eternal, sacrosanct and actionable.

Death is Life and Life is Death. Life culminates in Death and Death bursts forth in new Life. The inability of the senses to see beyond curtains does not curtail or hamper any activity that goes behind.

Theme 2 results in the Three Boons

1.1.7 Guru Nanak went under water for 3 days. Good Friday to Easter Sunday comprises of 3 days. Rome was not built in a day - but 3 days are more than sufficient to complete all tasks. Roka, Ring ceremony, Marriage. X axis, Y and Z. 3dimensional creation. say *annadātā sukhī bhava* thrice. SpaceTimeWarp. SeenSightSeer. NightDawnDay. LongWeekendDelight

so the story goes that for 3 days (as stated in following verse 1.1.9) i was in silence. (typical advance course format). no interaction. no eye-contact. away from media and smartphone. 3 days is the Laghu Shankh Prakshalan kriya in the Sri Sri Yoga Level two. Flushes out toxins. Makes the digestive fire radiant.

O Radiant. Visitor.
placate this Burning of his mind & emotions. O son of Sun (Death).

Theme 3 Patience, No Complaints

1.1.8 And the heavens exclaim! Fulfill his wishes. Attend to his needs. Nature bestows all upon the silent one. upon the patient one. when someone shows that extra grit and endures more than his normal capacity, all the great elements unite to do his bidding. his sufferings get wiped out.

Give your 110%. Go the extra mile with good cheer. be pleasant if you wish to conquer grief.

of puny awareness = lacking foresight

1.1.9 Since you have endured the trio of PastPresentFuture with great calmness, the King wishes you well.

You have displayed extraordinary grit during harsh summer, extreme winter and stormy monsoon. Since thee have balanced your tridoshas and trigunas, ask for any 3 choice boons.

Theme 4 Drop the Past

1.1.10 I make my first choice related to my PAST. i wish that my past mistakes be forgiven. i wish that i may rid myself of old bitterness and come to my PRESENT without a handicap.

May i live my present in equanimity. Of the three boons let this be my first.

1.1.11 The King wholeheartedly grants my first boon. He clears my dossier of previous imperfections and proclaims me fit and eligible for all present assignments.

Time and circumstances shall treat you without a handicap. Your debts have been cleared. Thee shall sleep in peace in the present without guilt, blame or agitation.

Theme 5 Heavenly life one's Birthright

1.1.12 to which i gleefully exclaim - O this is heavenly! O what life of the celestials, free from guilt, blame and fear! O the celebrities live without getting tainted by the media barbs, none can rob them of their fame, honor or luster. Their oomph and acceptability remain ever high.

Not there fear of laws or taxes, nor terror of old age.
Out of bounds for sorrow, no dearth of supplies, in the heavens one rejoices. O what a life!

Gratefulness erupts from the young lad. Gratefulness is the other name for abundant showering of Grace.

1.1.13 O Great King! Please teach me this skill.

Kindly impart me this quality of Brightness so that i too may GLOW and be welcome far and wide.

Consider this my request for the 2nd boon.

1.1.14 Granted. Thee shall have such a rare talent of being accepted sans borders. Thee shall travel without being questioned or frisked. This attribute is being etched in your DNA so you shall always have it.

1.1.15 Your chromosomes have been suitably restructured and imparted the Luminosity. You shall reflect like the Diamond and your Brilliance shall be your passport.

(in Sanskrit when a verse of utmost honor is being stated, it gets written in the third person, as a mark of acknowledging the handiwork of the Divine.)

Now, satisfied with himself, the King spoke further.

1.1.16 Pleased am i with thee and thankful am i to the Omnipotent. This new design and this new virtue and this new skill shall henceforth be christened after your name. Hereafter the SKILL of BRILLIANCE shall be called

"Nachiketa". The fastTag ID for use at toll-gates is henceforth named after you.

Let this be another medallion for thee sprung from my delight in your august company.

Accept this finely crafted Medal encrusted with precious gemstones that shall pave the way for whosoever gets drawn to you and is directed by you.

1.1.17 Whosoever gets trained in this faculty by you shall attain liberation. Whosoever seeks to imbibe this design in its entirety (the whole is represented by the number 3 - X.Y.Z. Sattva.Rajas.Tamas) shall cross over the frontier of fear. The one who unites his BodyMindSoul or the one who practices DharanaDhyanaSamadhi shall surely cross over this seemingly endless projection of creation.

1.1.18 He shall be hailed as the Wise. The practitioner of SANYAM thwarts all accidents and misfortunes.

No illness can touch him. No insult can taint him.

**His heart finds the truest LOVE.
in pleasing and comfortable environs. the earlier frustrating and blocking tendencies. having overcome. free of sorrows.**

1.1.19 As asked by you in 1.1.13, your second boon has thus been granted. Moreover, it has also been named after you.

Now please state your third wish.

Theme 6 My Innermost Wish

1.1.20 Gleefully i now voice my innermost desire. i say in all innocence - O King grant me the knowledge of Brahman. Remove my veil completely. Enlighten me to the Ultimate wisdom.

i ask since i have heard there is an omnipotent God. i have heard that there is something that is Imperishable. is it only a concept or is there something concrete? if what i have heard is correct grant me the union with the eternal Lord. Grant me Nirvana Mukti Moksha.

existence of life after death. regarding this much debatable-contentious-inconclusive topic. I your earnest disciple. this knowledge. grant as my third boon.

Theme 7 runs up the Road Block

1.1.21 O Nachiketa! This query of yours is profound. It is much too complicated. God is not exactly a transactable commodity. The intellect and one's reason fall short of such comprehension. Even the scriptures and scientists have shrouded it in mystery. Be generous not to press me over this point. Be kind to ask anything else except this.

this law is cryptic. Me don't pressurize. any other boon choose.

1.1.22 O King! so it is true that this is an unsolved mystery.
since you are the King and since the entire world
acknowledges thy supremacy, i think you are most
equipped to throw light on this subject. Grant me my WISH
that thee yourself rate to be the highest and most precious
in all the three worlds.

---

the King responded

Theme 8 Many Diversions Temptations

1.1.23 Take gold and silver and diamonds. Take any lands
you please and complete sovereignty over them. Take my
credit card and order each and everything listed on Amazon.
Buy any car, any spaceship, any villa, any MacBook. Marry
any maiden. Live for as long as you choose!

Now why would anyone offer Wealth instead of Wisdom?
Ponder deeply. Wealth is transient. It shall evaporate over a few
lifetimes. Most of us are content to give food in charity. Or cash.
How many of us take the Time and Effort to impart something
more durable like our skills and talents?

The Reason is simpler than one thinks. Time and Effort are in
short supply. That need lots of guts, planning and years of
quality input. Food and Cash are abundant and giving a small
percentage away is the easy way out. That is why the real Heroes
are those who are engaged in Education, Platform building,

Offering career choices and ensuring ways and means to give away the Eternal.

1.1.24 Likewise anything else strikes your fancy just bill it to me.

Choose Health Wealth Longevity Fame Power whatever.

I shall fix it so that even the most desirable girls will want thee.

1.1.25 Whatever object any man has attained in this world, i shall grant thee. The natural laws shall be at your service. The great elements shall manifest anything you need. Time shall keep you ever youthful and attractive.

Do not ask for Brahman. Do not ask for Ultimate wisdom. Let that remain a mystery.

Theme 9 however i Maintain Focus

1.1.26 But King these interest me naught. The worldly fancies do not attract me. My heart longs not for material goods nor for beautiful maidens.

TimeSpace and the creatures and events are but endless movies. Such trifles bother me not. Nature or its energies or man and his accomplishments are not what i seek.

1.1.27 O King! is it not your experience that Wealth keeps one hungering for more? Fame and power are never enough. the most desirable maiden too loses her attractiveness. Senses may get satiated but the mind keeps wanting.

I reiterate my innermost WISH. Grant me that alone as i shall not be swayed. Thee cannot tempt me O King!

1.1.28 All-knowing thou art O Great Emperor! You have the Highest Wisdom. How then can i ask for something less?

O Master! You are enlightened. Think thou that i shall bother thee with such petty matters as health, wealth, exam, marriage, job, relationships and the like? These things anyways we can get from your Secretariat, HODs, Ashrams, Schools, Yoga and Ayurveda centers and Society at large.

1.1.29 O King! I want to know what is the state of complete enlightenment? What happens to the Soul that has freed itself from this projected creation? What happens to the Actor who has played his part to such perfection that no further roles can be assigned to him - no more movies can be construed of to hold his stature since the entire cast and the sets pale in his presence?

O King! i wish to know the state of the man who wins all the gold medals in all the events of the Olympics? Certainly, no next Olympic or Competition dare field such a Hero again.

Since this is the deepest secret, never revealed, this is what i
Nachiketa ask for.

*The Great Emperor now begins his reply, being fully convinced
of the eligibility and determination of the disciple.*

Flower 1 Petal 2

The message of the Upanishad –
- Shreyas versus Preyas
- Plan long Term
- Your innermost Being is unknown to thee
- Shravanam-Mananam-Nidhidhyasanam
- OM is the Sacred Sound
- Qualify yourself

Theme 10 the Great Teaching

1.2.1 Know the grand fork in the road. the yonder well lit,
attractive, seductive and large sense gratifying limb is
known as the Preyas. The other plain, inconspicuous, least
ventured and rather unknown path is the Shreyas.

Most are drawn to the Pleasurable. Material comforts are a
priority for many. And certainly these are easy of
attainment. Whosoever applies himself a bit quickly ascends
the ladder of fame and fortune.

The unlikely and unknown and unadvertised is the Superior.

After all, how can one market the subtle that senses cannot grasp? The superior is totally unconcerned with bodily manifestations. Moreover, it lays no emphasis on intellectual skills.

Theme 11 Short Sightedness explained

1.2.2 As the logical gains of a single lifetime give no clue to the Superior, whereas the phenomenal rise to wealth and fame is quite evident, even the most intelligent do not deduce or put two and two together.

Mankind is used to living in partitions of lifetimes with no knowledge of the continuum, thereby he easily falls prey to the judgment of his senses or to the reasoning of his intellect. These faculties are quite limited in Time just as the body drops after a few decades.

Brave is the one who senses life after death. Brave is the one who embodies the wisdom of the 10 Gurus and sees them as One spanning 200+ years. Or the Gupta period known as the Golden Age lasting 200+ years. Or for that matter any period in history that outlives his lifetime. Or the common scientific knowledge that so many things in creation outlive man. Rare is the one who strives to keep on track no matter what, sensing for sure another life, sensing for sure his patience-perseverance-purity shall not be in vain.

1.2.3 O Nachiketa! Thee have pondered deeply. Thee have used Viveka to sift through the changeable and arrive at the unchanging. Thee have persevered where many have lost heart and gone astray.

Theme 12 the pleasurable ain't the Best

1.2.4 Avidya and Vidya are they so named, the Alluring and the Enlightening.

The first has limited domains. It is time and space bound. It is caught in a glass ceiling. It cannot see more than the obvious. As such it does not strive for the whole truth, being mired in one or more facets of the truth.

The other path is vastly different. The laws of nature weaken there. The great elements cannot perform in the rarer reaches. Time stops.

I am supremely pleased with thee Nachiketa. You cared naught for sensory pleasures or bodily attainments or intellectual fancies. Thee have amply demonstrated your fitness to transcend the Space Time dimension.

1.2.5 The materialists tend to get satisfied easily so their desires are more or less quenched by the ministers and office bearers or other clerks. They thus have no hope of audience with the King.

The glossy, gaudy, painted plastic trinkets who is attracted to has no hope of even knowing there is something called Gold. They who live thinking the sky is the limit have no clue to the infinity beyond.

Drinking only the white fluid from a plastic packet, they are foolish in believing they are having milk, since they really do not know about a vanishing species called the *desi gau* – A2 milk - that does not produce by the gallon. Also, it ain't milk if the calf hasn't been fed! Nor can properties of milk be determined *precisely* by mechanical instrumentation, so what to say of such follies or hair-brained wisdom.

1.2.6 And many such examples we see in all countries and cultures, where the essence gets shrouded in darkness and the gaudy gets flaunted and well accepted.

Nature hides its mysteries well and babes are those who think they have gotten the hang of anything.

1.2.7 The Truth is so hard, The Divine is so subtle, that it is extremely rare to hear of.

Having heard it doesn't make any sense. Reading the scriptures or listening to discourses makes no dent at all in the Avidya. The veil is bullet proof so as to say.

It is a wonder that some great saint appears on the landscape. It is a greater wonder that a fitting disciple is drawn to the satsang. And it is altogether a miracle that the wisdom finds its way in.

It is indeed extremely rare on this planet to have such a Teacher who speaks the wisdom and such a Student who actually hears it, understands and assimilates it.

1.2.8 The Guru who walks the talk is the realized one. The disciple who listens without distraction and wholeheartedly qualifies for the state of Yoga.

In fact words fall far short of the truth. the teaching happens on many planes, the central nervous system is still uncharted territory.

1.2.9 Scriptures when get spoken as pieces in between gossip or Discourses when analyzed from a lawyer's standpoint do not reveal themselves. Truth when emanating through divisive intellects, jaded channels or scholarly debates loses its potency.

O Nachiketa! one pointed indeed is thy focus. You epitomize the highest seeker. Blessed are the Masters whose disciples are like you.

Like you a Seeker none could be.

Theme 13 Brahman is Elusive

1.2.10 Brahman is an elusive goal. Brahman is so invaluable that none have it in their sights. No one even attempts to seek Brahman. After all who do you think seeks to be close-friends with the fiery sun? The brilliance of the sun shall in no time quell that emotion and deter that determination.

Supreme Bhakti is needed for such an umm-possible endeavor.

O Nachiketa! i too have performed Agnihotra with a devout

heart for a long time to attain to a celestial state. However, i fall far short of where you are headed for. Go on and attain the Ultimate. Fortunate am i that thee chose me for instruction.

1.2.11 O Nachiketa! i praise you again and again. i extol your resolve time and again.

What a vision thee have granted me. Through you i am also being showered by the abundant grace of Brahman. You have uplifted me to the point where i can experience that sweetest nectar that has no equal.

This Agnihotra, this Vaishvanara principle that has now been named after you as Nachiketas Agni, the granter of the celestial domain - has been skillfully bypassed by you for the highest. You have in one master stroke aimed for the unattainable Brahman.

I could only grant to thee the celestial life. However, by aiming for the farthest beyond, you have not only cleared your way for its achievement, nay you have also corrected my equation and given me back my boyish aim. i too shall now correct my course and having completed my current assignment shall put Brahman alone in my sights.

1.2.12 Brahman is the most elusive, completely hidden and rather easy to forget goal. That which is the cradle of all, that which is the blank screen on which all dramas are enacted, who can even have the faintest inkling of realizing it?

Deep in the heart's cave. Heart to signify that which has the wildest fancies, that can generate the craziest unthinkable incredible emotion. Heart to signify that which cannot be quenched. That you pour and pour into but never ever gets half filled. In the cavernous depths of the silent heart is Brahman.

Yoga is the way towards its attainment. A spiritual discipline like Sanyam can get you there.

Brahman is so still. so silent. so subtle. grief and glory, victory and defeat, loss and gain - O so shallow and clumsy are these phenomena in its presence! or even in its absence they are powerless.

Theme 14 Listen Ponder Assimilate

1.2.13 Having heard this, ponder over it, and assimilate it bit by bit. Shravana Manana Niddhidhyasana. this intimate note to the sincere seeker is his lighted pathway and also his resting quarters. whosoever hears this quintessential wisdom is fortunate in this world. whosoever treads this path of yoga surely finds peace in the heart.

O Nachiketa! the doors to liberation have been flung wide open for thee. Thee are being welcomed by Brahman.

1.2.14 O King! please continue your instruction. i am all ears. please talk of that which is beyond right and wrong. please talk of that which regards corruption and continence as mere children's playthings. please speak of the one who loves and supports all sans bitterness. please enlighten me to Brahman in whom we all merge and again emerge from.

Please say about the one where action and inaction meet. which is the cause of both matter and antimatter. that which consumes both galaxies and black holes. that which starts and stops time at will.

Theme 15 Om the Transcendental

1.2.15 Okay so listen. Brahman is personified by the syllable OM. Even though unutterable, by chanting Om you can experience Brahman. Om is the sound that does not need a medium. Om is the un-struck sound. Om is the bedrock of the visible and invisible creation. Om is the means and it is also the fruit. All words culminate in Om. The purpose of all scriptures is to enlighten this fact alone.

1.2.16 Om is aksharam the indestructible. Om is that which does not decay. Om reflects Brahman. Om points to Brahman and by Om merit accrues.

Who learns the essence of Om, he achieves all success. His life becomes a joy and his each moment becomes worthwhile.

Learn Om from a Master. Learn to chant from a gurukul. They will tell you to use Om as a prefix to some principle like "Om Namah Shivaya", "Om namo bhagavate vasudevaya" "Om Shanti Shanti Shanti". Om is a transcendental entity and for us mortal beings some principle like Auspiciousness, Prosperity, Peace etc. when added to it makes Om integrable, usable, transactable and beneficial.

1.2.17 This principle entails the highest good. The great one who integrates this law of Brahman in his life is revered by all.

He who practices this discipline achieves the final aim of all mortals - immortality.

1.2.18 Brahman is further glorified as the sacred space within each one of us that remains constant and untouched by time, phenomena, bodily transformations or any other means. Brahman is too subtle to be in any law's grasp. So it does not have the general attributes of birth and death and any corresponding features. *(refer Bhagavad Gita 2.20).*

1.2.19 Brahman is beyond the great elements so it does not change or fluctuate by altering their composition.

Hence those who reason or deduce from external sources or even from their own experience do not understand Brahman. Nor does anyone understand the qualities of Brahman since it is beyond Quality.

As an analogy consider a hologram that contains data. we are told that even when the hologram is cut or broken, the data remains intact.

(refer Bhagavad Gita 2.19).

1.2.20 Brahman is farther than thoughts can travel, it is far different from anyone's fantasy or imagination or science fiction.

Brahman is beyond reason, beyond volition and beyond anything else.

Brahman is neither vikalpa and nor is it sankalpa. Brahman is not desire and certainly it is not lack of desire.

The pleasant mind can reflect Brahman. A tranquil state can experience Brahman. That coincides only by grace.

1.2.21 Like the air it is everywhere. Air moves as breeze or as a storm, yet it fills all void simultaneously. None can choke or suffocate or even get too much of it, since Brahman cannot be addressed by such finite descriptions.

We might say Brahman is the light but even that does not do it justice being insufficient.

O Self! only you know this sacred space. i struggle with words, descriptors, pointers, analogies; none adequate, none close to the truth.

1.2.22 A tenacity is needed to get the grace of Brahman. Brave heart, large heart, never-say-die spirit distinguishes the rare one who gets showered by nectar.

Brahman is the out of body experience. Brahman is an out of the world experience. A state that has no parallel.

1.2.23 Brahman cannot be the subject of discourse, nor of reason, nor philosophy. Brahman can only be sought from the intensity of one's being.

To the sincere seeker Brahman comes as his own unique experience. It is not a template. It is not code. It is not a mantra. It is a sort of revelation. Eureka.

1.2.24 Even so the wicked are not known to have the revelation. The cruel, barbaric, sensuous or treacherous minds have never experienced such grace.

If there is a change of heart however the probability resurfaces. Those who mend their ways also stand the chance.

Theme 16 Qualifications are a Must

1.2.25 The Bhaktas and the Gyanis and the fearless Brave are the most qualified to attain Brahman. This Space Time domain is but a leaky projection that is tangential to the source.

How then may the ordinary non-striving souls ever deduce of its magnificent existence?

The Lord shines forth in this world through the acts of the pure souls who may be in any vocation. We can only surmise they are the fortunate whose life has been a shining example to humanity.

Flower 1 Petal 3

The message of the Upanishad –

- The Body must be well Driven
- Purity-Peace-Love qualify your Being
- Meditation is the Key

---

in the body. of good deeds. the essential truth. the two who get nourished. in the divine. abode. deep within. (both) entered.

both = Shiva and Shakti. Purusha and Prakriti. Witness and the Doer. Simply the Dual nature of Creation is hinted at.

1.3.1 O qualified Seeker! now hear this supreme secret of manifestation of Brahman on to the canvas of creation. Firstly, Brahman differentiates into the subtle and the gross. Both appear simultaneously in the deep recesses of the heart - antahkarna.

One is the light and the other is the reflection. one is the color and the other is the colorless. one is the proton and other is the electron. However, do not form any opinion or notion of high-low, superior-inferior or the like. Do not make any comparison. Do not form a judgment.

Words for describing Brahman are mere thought receptacles. They cannot give anyone the true understanding. It will only be your self-effort and sincerity on the path that will illumine the truth to you.

The practitioners of the Panchagni Meditations and the

performers of the trikaal sandhya Agnihotra rituals have glimpsed the Brahman and spoken to us.

Panchagni meditation techniques have been extensively described in the Patanjali Yoga Sutras as various Sanyam techniques. These are also the subject matter of Vigyan Bhairav. Of course all Upanishads also give Meditation keys and panchagni is simply a common term to contemplate on 5 desires. Pentagon is a geometric representation of fire. Fire means desire, determination or aim that has an evolutionary pathway.

The PANCAKOSHA Meditation is one of the famous techniques of panchagni vidya. Also, the caring for five societal instruments by any earning citizen – viz. birds and bees, cows and animals, guests or passersby, temples or public places, and the bright and intelligent children.

Consider a hypothetical equation. we can list 5 basic theories. - A = b. a =/ b or a and b cannot be meaningfully compared. a > b. a< b. a ~ b.
Consider another scenario.
why was i born? when will i die? did i exist before birth? what is my state if any after death? are these four cases applicable to me only, or some, or all (where all includes animate and inanimate).?
Such Meditations are termed Panchagni and form the backbone of any spiritual practice or tradition.

Similarly to throw some light on Nachiketas Agni done thrice. the day has three parts - day, twilight, night. Or we can say there are 3 meeting points in a day - dawn, noon, dusk. Any being performs 3 basic functions - eating, sleeping, working. (for many entertainment is a part of eating or sleeping or working so not listed separately).

The Sudarshan Kriya is magical as it fits both Panchagni and also Nachiketas Agni. Sudarshan Kriya has 5 distinct components - Pranayama, Bhastrika, Om Chanting, Rhythmic breathing and Relaxation. Sudarshan Kriya has 3 stage pranayama. 3 rounds of Bhastrika. 3 times Om chant ...

1.3.2 May the devout aspirants learn and practice Nachiketas Agni.

May the sincere seeker aspire for Liberation. May they attain the highest fruit of crossing over the frontiers of fear.

Theme 17 the Great Ship

1.3.3 A beautiful allegory is portrayed here. Our body is the perfect vehicle, the best spaceship it is. Our mind that is continuously spewing forth thoughts is the gearshift. our intellectEducationExperience is our captain or commander or driver. and mySelf that is hidden even from me (practically unknown to me or even to anyone else) is what is enjoying the failures and successes of the journey.

1.3.4 The wise say that Our senses are the controls and meters, the entire instrumentation. The paths and trajectories travelled are quite influenced by the instrumentation. And the spoils of the victories and tests cleared and positions attained are equally shared by the being-body-mind complex.

senses (are like) wild-horses they said.
objects like wayward paths. sum-total the experiencer. The
wise said.

1.3.5 Unwise is he who drives in a vehicle that is not clean, tire pressure not even, fuel and fluids not checked. For sure his instrumentation will be awry, his ship will get easily buffeted, his intellect will be mighty confused and his journey prone to failure.

1.3.6 Successful is he whose ship is well maintained, doubly checked for balancing and alignment and crisp instrumentation. His steering will be deft and decisive.

1.3.7 Unsuccessful is he who chooses to be lazy, wayward and prone to sense gratification. How can his ship get even near the midway mark?

Even if he seems to be rolling in wealth, in no time will his merit be exhausted; punctured his car will stutter to a stop, surely his ship shall stall.

1.3.8 The Meritorious talented advance step by step. They achieve fame gradually and then grace draws them over the finish line.

1.3.9 And the conscientious hard working proceed with patience and perseverance. The forces of nature aid them and they too get showered by grace finally.

1.3.10 Stronger than sensory inputs are the individual perceptions or tolerances for each sensation. These are stored differently in each of our brains. Stronger than perception is the toughness of the mind, or the thoughts resulting from the meeting of sensations and perceptions. Again this mental fitness is of a different quality for each one of us.

Then we are told that Reason or Intellect or Intelligence is superior to the mental faculty. Finally the indwelling soul or sacred space is the strongest of all parts. It means that the course of evolution or success achieved by an individual can be analyzed by his internals. *(refer Bhagavad Gita 3.42).*

1.3.11 Stronger than the embodied Soul is the cosmic Soul (or sum together of souls). And beyond the cosmic soul is that Brahman also known as Purusha.

Man must sift these faculties with great discrimination. Bit by bit with Kriya and Sanyam he must strengthen each so that the Purusha emerges as his target.

Theme 18 Purity Peace Love

1.3.12 Purusha = Brahman = Soul = Purity = Peace = Love filters through each component of the bodyMind complex. It is available in all though it may not be evident as its nature is to be hidden.

This verse is a heart stopper. After differentiation comes Integration. Such is the beauty of the Upanishad. (see Bhagavad Gita 7.25).

Why is this verse so IMPORTANT?
Simply because at the end of the day, at the bottom line it reinforces the saying LOVE is RULING this creation. PURITY is in charge. This thought is so powerful that it has been the INSPIRATION for countless human beings. It is the bedrock of NATURE. It is what makes our pet animals a delight. It fills our FOOD with rich taste. It makes plants and flowers and forests grow vibrant. It is evident in any WILD animal. It is the spontaneous JOY in every child.

This Verse or Verses similar to it in the Scriptures of the World is the backbone of SOCIETY. It is what keeps our civilizations going, our hopes high, our relationships strong, our work passionate and our entertainment casual.

Earlier in verse 1.3.11 we gave a different meaning to the soul and the purusha. That was to indicate a part of Brahman that is as if mesmerized by the body-mind-complex or so shaded. And the part of Brahman that is untouched.

Such techniques are used in the Upanishads to help smoothen the path for the Seeker. To keep up his faith and help him navigate through the various tantrums, storms and challenges. To reason with him logically so that the transition from the known to the unknown or from the finite to the infinite is enthusiastic and pleasant.

Theme 19 a Meditation Technique

1.3.13 A potent Meditative technique. Withdraw your attention from the body by sitting still and closing your eyes. After sometime attention will cease from the senses. Now withdraw the thoughts by not chasing or building upon them. After a while the random thoughts only shall remain. It means the intellect has been absorbed or is no longer functional.

This is a very profound meditative technique and gives remarkable results. As the mind becomes quiet, the breath becomes steady and subtle. Conversely, as we breathe slowly and deeply, the thoughts become sparse and random.

Now those wishing or capable of sitting for longer duration can practice merging themselves into the space around. Slowly one loses body awareness. Slowly one becomes ONE with the supreme consciousness. Finally, even this notion of unity drops. There is deep stillness.

This is called merging into the Brahman. This is how the Saints live. That is why they radiate so much Love. So much Peace follows in their wake.

1.3.14 ARISE Awake O dear one! Go to the best schools. Qualify to apply to the top ranked colleges. Get a proper and complete education. They shall nurture your budding talents. They shall make you worthy citizens of society.

Seek far and wide. Humbly request the Guru to take you under his guidance. You have been given a precious body. You have been endowed with enough dormant energies that are mightier than the biggest tsunami. Unless properly nurtured and carefully channelized they shall remain dormant or shall rise up uncontrollably to cut you apart like a fine razor's edge. This world is a labyrinth of endless pitfalls.

Leave no stone unturned to prepare and equip yourself for a noble HUMAN life.

Swami Vivekananda – "Arise Awake and Stop not till the Goal is Reached", inspiration from this Katha Upanishad verse.

1.3.15 Another powerful Meditation. Contemplate on THAT which has no sound. Think of the ONE without touch form taste or smell. i.e., Sit still and withdraw your senses bit by bit.

Soon you shall not hear the passing traffic. Conversations around you shall fade away. Even unexpected knocks and bells shall not catch your attention.

Then dwell on the idea of changelessness. See your own self as unchanged. See your home and city as continuing far into the future. See this creation as vast, diverse, without frontiers. Feel the infinity all around.

Such is the power of Meditation that it shall snap your sanchita karma. It will wipe away your old scars and blemishes. It will also prevent further trauma or unsavory impressions. Meditation will make you sound and your talents shall sprout forth.

Meditation clears the doubts and suspicions and mental

haziness. It makes the intellect free of guilt and rescues the heart from hatred. Thus, it allows the body to rid itself of illness easily.

1.3.16 Anyone who has the good fortune to listen to this dialogue between the young boy Nachiketa and Grandfather Time attains success in this life.

Also if someone reads this story or recites the verses or does these meditations, he gets freed from afflictions and is prevented from grief.

Such a soul is hailed by the gods as the intelligent one worthy of His grace.

1.3.17 This very potent, precious, practical yet elusive wisdom has been enumerated in this Upanishad in the form of a story Katha.

Such knowledge is indeed hard to find and harder still to ingrain.

Whosoever is passionate about spreading wisdom (as a Professor), whosoever arranges for the flowering of wisdom (as running a School), and whosoever takes it upon himself to learning the wisdom (as a sincere student); they all achieve merit, success and noble standing in this creation.

That is a Guarantee. Certified herewith.

Flower 2 Petal 1

The message of the Upanishad –

- Grass is greener on the Other Side
- Seek proper Counsel
- Describing the Indescribable

Further elaboration of life, society, communities and thoughts follows.

Great Nature. outward. holes, sensors.

Theme 20 Nature of the Senses

2.1.1 The supreme Brahman wishing to foster relationships made our senses take notice and appreciate the beauty around us. The worldly phenomena became exciting and people felt attraction for each other. Thus mankind evolved to build strong city states.

A few brave and exceptional souls however kept their eyes averted and turning within got absorbed in the source of it all. They tasted a bliss that was far superior to the highly paid actors and the famed celebrities.

outwardly. pleasures. run after. they fools. widespread. of frustration and sorrow. tentacle, grip. are caught.
on the other hand. the patient brave. inviolable. nectar. having experienced. in the temporal. herein. not. are drawn to.

Theme 21 Guru comes to the Rescue

2.1.2 They the great actors, builders, scientists and administrators at some point in their life meet some realized soul and immediately feel puny, childish and humbled. Their transcendental pathway opens and they get diverted in the nick of time from the vortex of impending doom.

Transitory it has been stated for all the materialist attractions only because the capacity of our senses is finite and our bodies cannot really indulge beyond a certain limit. After having experienced success in worldly pursuits a void or plateau looms ahead that is scary and unending.

To rescue these travellers who toil hard and long the Saints manifest and teach effortlessness and relaxation. The saints are perfected beings who have known the outer and the inner. They have come to the conclusion that there is an external universe of SpaceTime and its rigid laws that pales in comparison to the ever blissful frontier less Brahman.

Theme 22 the Way of Brahman

2.1.3 By whose grace the varying shades and smells, strains and colors are experienced. By whom one is led to feel attraction and revulsion, hope and despair, isn't that verily bigger than the manifest?

Once the thought goes towards the Director of the grand play, a subtle crack in the glass cage develops letting in the fragrance of freedom.

This is the Brahman. This is That which is the most precious.

___

2.1.4 It is by the will of Brahman that we see the world as solid when awake and experience the dream as real when asleep.

The intelligent brave is one who has tasted the Brahman and so bland the sensual delights for him have become.

___

2.1.5 And so also having known the future as a reflection of the past, fear has evaporated from his heart.

The pain and grief and disgrace do not deter him one bit, so he welcomes them all, shying from none.

This is Brahman. This is that most sought after.

___

2.1.6 There is something that came before the beginning. There is an entity that is the source of focus or discipline or strength or any virtue.

There is an invisible force that powers the wind and rides the storm. Since no one has discovered its secret, since it is so well hidden, It is the Brahman.

This is That the deepest longing.

___

2.1.7 There is a sap permeating the creation that moves each star, wills each thought and fuels each burst of emotion.

This that immerses the matter, that which soaks in the antimatter, the one hidden so deep in one's heart that it gushes forth only in extreme peril.

This is Brahman. This is That which makes us shine.

2.1.8 Fire is hidden in each twig. Oil is encapsulated in every seed. Life throbs in the pregnant, so it is said a tender heart holds the Brahman.

The wise perform meritorious deeds and attribute it all to its glory.

This is Brahman. This is that which makes us talented.

2.1.9 O see yonder such handsome boys, and those beautiful girls going about. Who do you think lends them grace and infuses desirability in their movements?

All the great and the noble to whom owe their greatness; That none surpasses.

This is Brahman. This is that unrivalled pizzazz.

2.1.10 What is in Him is also in Her and so it is vice versa. What is Here in a blade of grass is also There in yonder tree. Open your eyes and see the same magic in every win and in every ruin.

Then can you overcome your weakness; nay drop your blames forthwith.

2.1.11 They say of a crazy mind that delves the mystery. Only that one solves the riddle and escapes unscathed.

Yet many keep losing themselves in the maze of their emotions. Many keep getting frustrated and remain caged in their petty worlds.

The reality escapes them while Brahman maintains amity.

2.1.12 Senses the rare of the subtle in some fleeting moment. That merges both his past and his future so he rises above defense.

This is Brahman. This is that which frees the Soul.

2.1.13 Imagine the improbable and you will get close. Travel back in time and see it is innocent and auspicious. Bolster hope that future's bright.

This is Brahman. This is that known as faith.

He Lord of the Past-Present-Future. He alone today and also tomorrow.

2.1.14 Each has been granted a gift. Each has been endowed with a uniqueness.

Focus on your strength, sharpen your skill, play your own part; lest you diffract, scatter and get wasted.

2.1.15 O Gautama! When you stand firm the dust settles. When you take responsibility nature blesses. When you prime the pump, the water gushes.

Purity begets Purity.

So does the Soul merge in Brahman having done its duty, having

given its 100%.

as when in clear. clear water. is added and mixed. as that only. it becomes. of the all-knowing wise person. soul. gets fully absorbed (in Brahman.)

Flower 2 Petal 2

The message of the Upanishad –

- There is Math in Creation
- Prana Apana the Vital Airs
- Describing the Indescribable

Theme 23 there is Math in Creation

2.2.1 Eleven doors to a structure form the minimalistic design. One each for the five elements to be cognized. One each for the five motor functions. Apart from these ten physicals, an eleventh has been stated to account for intuition or extra sensory perception.

Structures possible include a human body, a school, a gated city, a nation state or a vehicle. In the case of a state, core depts. could be 1 home 2 finance 3 education 4 agriculture 5 industry 6 transport 7 irrigation 8 Defense 9 external affairs 10 human resources and 11 information. In the case of a vehicle, functional attributes can be 1 tire 2 fuel 3 ac 4 sensors 5 lights 6 doors 7 steering 8 chassis 9 engine 10 gears 11 seats.

A school can make sense with academics, music, sports, faculty, students, registrar, exams, transport, picnics, crafts and astronomy.
A home can have Verandah, Terrace, Lawn, Backyard, Bedroom, Kitchen, Bath, Hall, Garage, Study, Meditation areas.

Success in a new design or blueprint or construction shall hinge on taking care of 11 concepts. Plan your business with completeness. Plan your education likewise. Then you are assured of regret free operation.

This is Brahman. This is that holistic design.

2.2.2 Eleven attributes of manifest creation and its associated energies from the Rig Veda are glorified. Celestial space. Atmospheric cover. Earthly plane. Flora. Fauna. Mountains. Rivers. Oceans. Food chain. Eco system. Mineral wealth. and changing seasons.

The great truth has eleven facets. The complete truth is multidimensional. Give due respect to all since all is pervaded by Brahman.

Theme 24 Prana Apana Vital Airs

2.2.3 A living organism consists of breath moving inwards and down i.e., accumulation of skills and possessions and family; and outwards and up i.e. maturity and balance and stature.
There is a sense of individuality and it is honored by society.
Meditate on this deeply. Watch the Breath.

2.2.4 For the one aspiring to be great, minimum attachments are entailed, so that the exit is clean, swift and evolutionary.

Brilliance is ever that system of clean plug and play. Design that is backwards compatible and totally futuristic.

This is Brahman. This is that which evokes awe.

2.2.5 However life is not only about designing and planning, or in coming and going. It isn't only about sensations and emotions. Nor becoming fat or fit.
Life is also the steadfast and the unmoving. Life was perfect in the beginning and remains so in the end.

2.2.6 O Gautama! Now i shall detail the mechanics of sound design and good strategy. A proper design is one that will not need revision. Changes and Revisions are the direct result of faulty, hurried or corrupt mentality. If one needs to change job or house or spouse at a frequency more than a rarity, it simply points to an unsatisfactory schooling and an imbalanced constitution.

This is an undesirable state of clay that is brittle, a raw material that continues to be volatile. We can clearly say - divinity is missing, Brahman is lacking - but in fact it is something mysterious. A longer, insipid unflattering journey, odyssey nevertheless.

2.2.7 Who can say what a Samsung S10 smartphone is thinking? What are the imaginations of a Boeing Dreamliner jet? Do they also will a better life? Does the sprawling city also dream of innovative bridges, cutting edge buildings and accident-free zones?
It is all dependent on the Creator's will. The Director's mind can take any turn and fashion any set.

2.2.8 Someone else is doing the fine tuning. Some hidden propulsion is also at work. Your mind is nudged, tacked, deflected or guided by an invisible device it is often felt.

This is Brahman. This is that which ensures an ending of it all.

2.2.9 The grid powers all cities. The grid kicks it all alive. Light manifests as a bulb or a knife or the idea in a coconut - whether to become tasty chutney or triangular barfi or remain plain white.

Don't get caught up in these expressions, salute the fire

within.

2.2.10 The breath moves in each being. Atmosphere is
breath, the wind is breath and so is the deadly tsunami.

Start the practice of Pranayama as it regulates the outer
forces and balances the inner desires leading to
spectacular results.

---

by the miseries of the world. that which cannot be touched
being far away. the one all-pervading truth deep inside.

2.2.11 Have you observed that the Sun is unaffected by
thunder and lightning and the dustiest storm? Such is the
quality of a great Soul who maintains élan, responsibility
and functionality in the face of trials and tribulations that
visit every being on this planet.

Grit, tenacity, titiksha and uparati are the pathways to
international success. Success that transcends culture,
religion, region and generation.

2.2.12 Have you observed a baby's pull on each family
member, nay neighbor and stranger? The baby is brimming
with raw energy; an undirected, unmediated enthusiasm.
All of us including animals and plants have it in varying
degrees though it has become cracked, tracked and
trackable.

A baby's is untracked or unlimited. That is why we get
infected by a baby's charm and it is this Brahman that is

strongly evident here.

It is the Brahman that bubbles forth in each and every baby. It is the Brahman that makes anything or anyone inviting and interesting and exciting.

And it sure doth manifest in each being. A saint's eye notices it and thus he alone maintains tranquility, peace, bliss.

2.2.13 And further a Saint also notices the smelly, decrepit, foul traits of each being, but he pays it scant attention. For he is so much absorbed in the Beauty. He is so much soaked in the Brahman, that the non-Brahman-if-any is non-existent for him.

Notice that ungodliness, wrong-hood, or any such words are just that. Words without substance. Or to put it another way, some dust or gloom that has come our way as a stepping stone to great success.

Lasting happiness is his alone who cultivates a scientific temper.

Theme 25 Acceptance-Sanatana Dharma

2.2.14 The master stroke follows. How am i to say what is Brahman and what it is not? Who am i to give the law or lay the code of conduct?

I laugh at myself and wonder at what i speak. Infinity is thy name and infinite are your ways. My definition of infinity is at best an opinion that is easily replaced by better men. By anyone since "better" is again my viewpoint.

So i concede my thinking is Brahman-speak and also those at variance are Brahman-speak.

not expressible in words. ultimate bliss. how can anyone discern?
how and upon whom grace is bestowed, specially granted or not.

Theme 26 O Beautiful!

2.2.15 Where the sunlight doesn't reach. Where no moonbeams venture forth. Not even galactic dust is reflected.

Where lightnings don't put up road shows. Where a thing as Fire is unheard of un-struck.

No it is not any black hole nor any anti matter nor an indescribable universe. Rather it is that which spins the dreams and manifests it all.

It is the one that tingles, surprises, nourishes, excites, takes tender loving care.

there sunlight reaches not.
nor starlight.
how then could this firelight?
All is lit by that alone.
of its light this all is lit.

Such contemplation leads to profound Meditation.

100 Katha

Flower 2 Petal 3

The message of the Upanishad –

- Discern the changing Duality
- Use the 5 fingers and 5 senses responsibly
- Use the 6th sense
- To realize the Ultimate

Theme 27 Duality Dvaita

2.3.1 Know the Brahman as the summum bonum of duality. Know it as the opposing forces in equilibrium. Know it as both right and wrong. (see Bhagavad Gita 15.1). Know it as eternally transitory.

We surmise history to be some few thousand years old. We calculate and speculate. We change our perception and understanding every few decades.

We keep on discovering and inventing. Earlier we are so sure it is improbable, then it becomes so commonplace that we summarily reject its occurrence before its current invention.

Each newness fades into oblivion, yet science freezes its lifespan in a start and stop date. Then someone discovers yet another state.

Even though timeSpace appears one way in the waking, the dream comes and turns it topsy turvey.

2.3.2 Logic is designed to follow some course, but emotions erupt to smash all courses. A teen behaves one way under supervision or surveillance and completely unexpectedly elsewhere.

A boss who can see through logic and emotion, who can reconcile the trustworthy and the unreliable, verily he becomes the Top Boss.

lots of respect for the wondrous phenomena. such their understanding.

Theme 28 the Magic of FIVE

2.3.3 The great elements five in number. Babytime-studenthood-livelihood-marriage-retirement five in number.

Typical administrative zones
East/West/South/North/Center.

5 fingers and 5 senses. The fives are just a relative notion and yet assume permanent significance.

Authority will involve an element of Fear.

2.3.4 A man who can develop his sixth sense, laughs at follies and forgives easily.

He who incorporates Meditation easily rises above mental voltage fluctuations. And maintains sanity in old age and departs with good cheer.

2.3.5 At babytime there are no limitations or notions. In student life some vague tracks start forming in the brain. In professional life the big notions take concrete shape. In wedded life many lifelong promises are made.

After retirement one sees manifestation of most dreams through children and grandchildren or even through their better halves.

2.3.6 One may even compare the 5 stages in time to the simultaneous yet different workings of the 5 faculties viz. breath, senses, intellect, memory and intuition.

The brave is able to reaffirm his own identity in each stage of life and in each functioning faculty. Thus there is no fear, no hatred thus no grief.

Theme 29 the 6th Sense or Intuition

2.3.7 Strongly rule us the Breath, the Senses, the Intellect, the Memory, yet Intuition has the ultimate say.

2.3.8 Far higher than individual intuition is the intuition of Time and Space. This is invisible, indefinable, without parallel.

The far-sighted gets a glimmer of Eternity's handiwork and is thus not afraid of failure, or disgrace or exiting from the bodily plane.

2.3.9 Eternity is hard to catch in a rearview mirror, nor is it visible in the headlight. Eternity does not display sensory tentacles, but the great thinker through studious contemplation arrives at its presence in the deep recesses of his brain.

This Sanyam who practices overcomes delay in realizing his goals since Eternity has become his bosom friend.

2.3.10 When one's breath has become subtle, the senses have become un-distracting and the mind has become calm; know that state to be the Ultimate.

2.3.11 The wise call it Yoga. Sanyam is another name.

Know that Yoga is not taking it for granted, it is neither carelessness, nor is it lethargy.

A yogic state has a depth, maturity and stability that is long-lived. It is a seamless state endowed with viveka-vairagya-titiksha-uparati-shraddha and samadhan.

It is not escaping the dangers, rather a skill in dealing with danger.

2.3.12 Surely the materialist world is not equipped to instruct in all aspects of the functioning of the mind. At best it can teach survival, and it can get us name and fame.

The world's schools do not equip us with protection from depression, frustration, guilt, shame, or any other major pitfall. The best colleges do not have any means to safeguard as from the most abysmal vices nor prevent even intelligent minds from becoming depraved, rotten or corrupted. Even the simple and most honored virtues of truthfulness, sincerity, forgiveness, patience and kindness are neither encouraged nor enforced in any institution.

But you may well ask, of what use are these when they are not in demand? My friend at one point in life you shall stand at the crossroads. That fork shall come and it might be too late then. Perhaps to many the fork comes in some other lifetime, but the Upanishad says we must prepare whenever we can for a life of purity, for a life of joy, for one of complete freedom.

2.3.13 Focus on the greater dimensions of Existence. Understand the principles underlying this Creation. Make the Ultimate your passion. Make the hardest your target. That vision yields the best results. Such a mission is what makes saints revered and welcome everywhere. It is the one aim that can be said to make the Lord happy and take notice.

deep desires. Ingrained notions. firmly anchored. get released.

2.3.14 When your entire fiber unites in pursuing Yoga. When a suppleness and melting has begun in the heart.

Know that to be the beginning of immortality.

Know that you shall achieve freedom. Know that you shall have no lack.

all knots of the heart. All the stored-up wounds, grievances, false impressions. in totality. instruction in self-discipline. Teaching of character-based lifestyle.

2.3.15 When the glass cage cracks open. When the stream of gratitude gathers momentum. When your heart no longer harbors suspicion.

When your sight has cleared and your fists have unclenched. When doubt and ill-will have been vanquished, know you have become Brahman.

Know you have reached your goal.

This is the Upanishad. This is the Teaching.

Theme 30 GO FOR IT

2.3.16 This Upanishad is practicable. This goal is achievable. Use the method of Yoga to make your mind laser like. Use the Breath and Meditation techniques to harmonize all thoughts, sift your emotions, and let the topmost priority out of the hundred and one lukewarm flings take center stage.

Then alone is the Olympic gold within reach. Then is the Divine fully realized.

2.3.17 The path is subtle and seldom trodden. There are many distractions on the way. The last mile becomes tricky, slippery, rather dull and insipid. Have patience, keep up the endurance, be brave and falter not. Do not give up. Give in not.

You should know the precious nectar is close. Your focus
should be on the eternal brilliance. Victory is to be had.
Freedom is surely yours.

in entirety. Fully. Wholesome. Brahman.
Yoga practice. Discipline of senses. A healthy lifestyle. Spiritual.
That which strengthens. never say die spirit.

2.3.18 This is how the young lad sat on his great
grandfather's lap and succeeded in imbibing the decisive
Wisdom.

Anyone who with faith and determination follows likewise
shall also attain Brahman. Immortality. Nirvana.

And what is this IMMORTALITY? It is being unafraid of
death. It is being not bothered by doubts, fears, suspicions.
It is being able to live guilt free, blame free, frustration free.
It is being able to be committed towards one's goals and at
the same time have a LOVING caring family.

It is going to SLEEP peacefully and soundly.
It is snapping out from the PAST.

END

4 The Mandukya Upanishad

Shanti Mantra

oṃ bhadraṃ karṇebhiḥ śṛṇuyāma devāḥ | bhadraṃ paśye
mākṣabhir yajatrāḥ | sthirairaṅgais tuṣṭuvāṃsastanūbhiḥ |
vyaśema devahitaṃ yadāyuḥ || svasti na indro vṛddhaśravāḥ
| svasti naḥ pūṣā viśvavedāḥ | svasti nastārkṣyo ariṣṭanemiḥ
| svasti no bṛhaspatirdadhātu || oṃ śāntiḥ śāntiḥ śāntiḥ ||
O Divine Wisdom! May our ears listen to the sacred and the
auspicious. May our eyes see the propitious as we come
together to partake of wisdom.
May our limbs be firm and body attuned to long endurances.
May our senses function with full alertness and
May the sense of contentment be strong.
May our good thoughts form a discus to shield us and May
our education give us a shining personality.
Peace in our heart, in our body and in our environs.

Mandukya is from the Atharva Veda. It elucidates the four
topics; Waking state, Dreaming State, Deep Sleep state, and
the ever present yet seldom knownTranscendental state.

Verse 1 OM is ALL

Om. Full stop. This imperishable it all (is);
of it. relative description. the Past Present Future.
this all Om Sound alone (is).
Moreover (adverb). / Other than (adjective). beyond the
concept of time. That which does not belong to a time
domain.

1 This world is a light and sound show. All of it here is just name and form. Each movie, app or game is two dimensional - audio and video.

Light can easily be shut by dropping the eyelids or covered by an eye-scarf. It is sound that has a bigger dimension that can't be just warded off.

Close your eyes and listen. Be still and let the waves speak. Become aware of the breeze whispering. Hark and hear the heartbeat, know it is a pulse.

This creation pulsates day and night. As the stars twinkle the biggest heroes get known by their one-liners and administrators by their quotable quotes.

Know this is all Om. Know it all as Aum. When a baby is born Om is heard and when bells peal, they chorus Aum. Ever since the bow of Space strung the arrow of Time, Om reverberated.

Om is manifest yet unmanifest too. Aum is the seed and the sprout and also the space and the sunshine.

Aum has been chanted in homes and workplaces. Om is the octave and Aum is the harmonic. Om is and will be.

Verse 2 ayam ātmā brahma

All verily this Brahman (is).
This Soul Brahman (is).
(all) That, (and) This Soul, four states (has).

Note. We have a masculine stem, that declines as Brahma

in the nominative. It has a different meaning as well.
Brahman (unqualified) is the invisible source of everything,
whereas Brahman (masculine) is a visible manifestation
and a particular facet of Brahman (unquantified) l

ayam ātmā brahma – A MAHAVAKYA

Termed in Vedantic lore as a Mahavakya, a
statement that is most powerful in the meditative
techniques. A statement that unlocks the secret of
creation. A statement that leads one to
transcendence. That has the force to overcome
misery.

# ayam ātmā brahma
soul = God
this being = the Lord
isness = the Lord
this itself = Brahman

2 Know it by another name too. Brahman. The Eternity.
Soul. The Center. with 4 spokes. rests on 4 pillars. has 4
expressions. 4 modes of transaction.

Close your eyes and know you are the Father and the
Flame, also the Son and the Stranger.

You are known at Home and in the Workplace. You are also
known in the Game and in the Temple.

Verse 3 Awake the Emperor

the one in waking state. the one with outward senses and attention. the seven limbed. the one with nineteen attributes. enjoyer of the gross physical stuff. world emperor. first. phase.

3 Your first expression is Wakefulness. All senses streaming. Memory and Intellect in strong positioning.

While awake you may not be alert. You may be tired and dull. You may be in stupor, panic, hallucination or wonder! There is a chance you are day dreaming without your knowledge!

Aims and Ambitions govern the *waker*. Me and Mine mark his boundaries.

The waking state is a reflection. It is bound by the intelligence, the education, the resources and the responsibility. It is bound by the body and its limits in the space time continuum. It is bound by the mind and how far it can soar.

Vaishvanara or state of processing all inputs. In computer language - Booted up state.

19 = 10+9 = 20-1. (1+9 = 10, 1+0 = 1 = Brahman = Turiya or transcendental state). One is the first number and Nine the last in a decimal set, and Nineteen is the 8th prime number. Our meditations are mostly 19-20 minutes. Potassium also known as Kalium, that is indispensable for living cells, has the atomic number 19. 19 can be written symbolically in various ways, e.g.,1,6+3 (163 figures in Ramanujan constant). 1,1+8. (118 eighteen means victory in Sanskrit). The Metonic cycle is 19 years.

Verse 4 Dream the Spark

the one in dream state the one with senses shut. the seven limbed one. the one-less-than-twenty faceted. enjoyer of the unmanifest subtle realm. the one with spark, i.e. looks inert but is actually alive. second phase.

a Taddhita derivative to mean the one with vigor. (even though in the dream state he appears inert).

4 Your second state is Dream. It is usually without sense input. More or less without memory and intellect functioning.

And how is that? In a sleeping dream most of us can be said to have switched off the senses, memory and intellect.

But for sure a few have these faculties on while dreaming. Latent desires sprout and take center stage. Cravings and Aversions rule the night.

What about the day dream? What about the fantasy and the building castles in the air? What about when you are imagining - as in a creative thought, or in illusion or even in a drugged state?

What about the Yogis or the ever wakeful?

The dream state surpasses the waking state. It has fewer limitations of body and mind. Where one might go in the dream can be another galaxy or somewhere in the Satya Yuga or far into the future.

This state is known to be the cause of numerous inventions! And why should it be superior to the waking? Simply because it is more easily forgotten and the slate is cleaner and dream impressions are more fluid than waking imprints.

Tejas or the state of being powerfully inactive. Standby.

Verse 5 Deep Sleep the Bliss

when the asleep one,
any desire not wills,
any dream not sees,
it deep sleep (is).

the one in deep sleep state the integrated one the solidified one like blissful Umm/Uhh the experiencer of bliss the conscious faced the sentient third phase.

5 Deep sleep is the third pillar. For sure senses are turned off. Intellect is off as well. Memory? Certainly, no memories in the way.

O such a delight it is to go to this state. So many yearn for sound sleep. How refreshing it is!

The body really needs it. Limbs get their restoration. The mind springs back to form after such deep rest.

Does anyone deny this state? Restarting, booting up mate. Even smart phones need it all the time.

Desires are thrown aside. Aversion and bitterness is forgotten.

Much sought for state. Many miracles and discoveries a deep sleep can anchor. Bleeding hearts can be stemmed, broken marriages repaired and so much love, forgiveness and awareness can result.

A deep Meditation is likened to deep rest. Since it restores innocence, confidence and clarity of vision.

Sahaj Samadhi Meditation is a natural and profound technique to achieve deep rest.

Restful. Blissful. Essential. Pragya is thy name.

Notice such a beautiful rendering of the three states or phases of living matter.

- *In the **wakeful** state, the being has been termed as the **Emperor**. In the sense of most resourceful, intelligent and powerful. Isn't this the way most of us go about?*

- *In the **dream** state, the being has been termed as the **one with a Spark**. In the sense that when one is dreaming, one usually appears inert and so this clarifies.*

- *In the **deep sleep** state, the being has been termed as the **Blissful one**. We have all noticed that anyone enjoying deep rest and contentment looks so divine and happy.*

Magic of 19

Various scriptures describe the human mind body complex using different numbers. The Bhagavad Gita uses the numbers 8 and 10 in different verses. The Vijnana Bhairava by Swami Lakshman Joo in its commentary of the 54th verse points to 36 elements in creation. Guruji also said this during Maha Shivaratri 2016 at Bangalore Ashram.

Out of these, one-less-than-twenty i.e. 19 facets can be culled on the physical plane: Bones-Muscles-Nerves-Organs-Fluids, five breaths, five senses, mind-intellect-ego-citta-SELF = 20 Minus ONE the SELF = 19.

A Centered Triangular Number given by $(3n^2+3n+2)/2$ results in 19 for n=3.

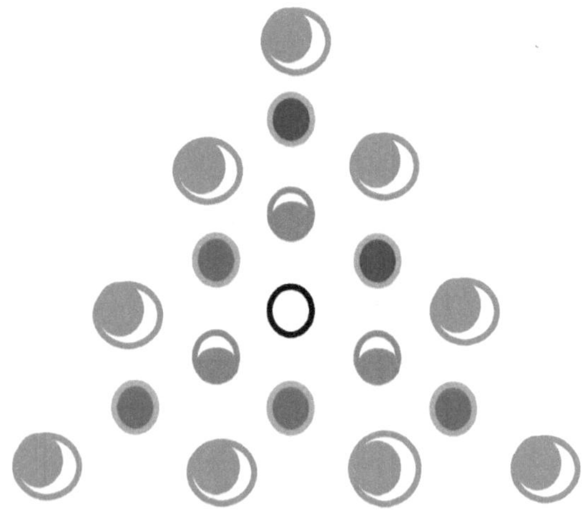

Verse 6 Ceaseless Change

it is the Lord of all and sundry. it is the all-knowing. it is the one deeply ingrained. of all it is the womb. of all sentient and non-sentient beings, moreover, it is the cause of birth and death / ceaseless change.

6 Who experiences these states? The soul within. The space within.

The divinity and the beauty that we all are made up of experiences Waking, Dreaming, Deep Sleep. That something which is alive inside.

Life is the experiment and the experience. The Actor is the act, the imagination and the stillness all rolled into one.

Do only humans go through the triad? Have you considered the flora and fauna? For sure all living beings go to sleep and wake up and move about. Perhaps some animals like the pet Alsatians also dream. May not be stretching it if one thought that Roses in the garden were scheming or that yonder Cloud was dreaming!

Verse 7 OM Brahman Neti Neti

They the wise regarding the 4th state opine,

(It is) not only sentient in the inside, not only sentient in the outside, cannot be said to be only sentient both inside and outside, not solidified, not consciousness, not unconsciousness.

(It is) not visible, not transactional, not graspable, not definable, not ponderable, not describable.

(It is) the essence of the experiences of the soul, the confluence of the great elements, peacefulness, auspiciousness, non-dual / not separable into parts.

that is the Soul,
that is to be understood.

7 Have you considered the foundations? The state that the other states rest upon? The state that cannot fit into the triad because it is too BIG.

Simply see your breath. Goes in. Comes out. And doesn't move at times. What about the switch from in to out? Or out to still?

Easily you are the Father and the Flame and the Son. But these three states are too well defined and sometimes you are the Stranger as well. When no one can define you.

Think about it. Ponder on that which is neither Time and neither Space and neither both. Contemplate on that which gave birth to time and space and remains untouched by both.

Is there something that is not matter and not anti-matter? For sure there is something that is beyond energy and matter. Beyond mind and emotion. Beyond the living and the non-living.

See the movie and become aware of the white screen. See the rope and wonder why it suddenly appeared to move. Is air alone the cause? Or did the gloomy weather and doubting mind conjure it up?

For sure there is more to than what meets the eye. There are lands and oceans where man has never ventured forth and not probed. There are galaxies where Newton's laws laugh and sing and keep changing. Where the math is so different a human intellect cannot divine.

This is the verse that is eulogized in Vedantic lore as **Not this. Not this...**

And it is so true. As one grows up, one drops old concepts. The best toys no longer interest. And slowly steadily when tries to express or explain the TRUTH, no words come. No words are adequate. No statements or explanations can deliver.

3 Aum Trīṇi

The number three looks very similar to the symbol OM, signifying its inherent triple quality. In Sanskrit, the number three is always in plural.

Verse 8 AUM = Waking Dreaming Sleeping

that imperishable Word Om this Soul (is). the phases
correspond to each letter. And the letters correspond to
each phase.
A-sound **U**-sound **M**-sound thus.

8 So what to do? Does it mean I shall never attain
Brahman? I shall never drop my past or my sorrow?

No No. Learn the proper way to chant. Learn the
mahavakyas and the mahamantras from the Master.

The Guru teaches that the sacred syllable AUM must always
be used as a prefix to other auspicious sounds.

e.g.
Om Namah Shivaya.
Om Namo Bhagavate Vasudevaya.
Om Hare Rama Hare Rama, Rama Rama Hare Hare, Hare
Krishna Hare Krishna, Krishna Krishna Hare Hare.
Om Namo Narayanaya…

And then the magic unfolds. The letters of the sacred
syllable infuse and impregnate one's consciousness with the
trinity that is LOVE JOY ENTHUSIASM. One's prana begins to
flow correctly and one's chakras open up one by one.

Verse 9 A-Wake = the Emperorship

the wakeful state termed as Vaishvanara = Emperor

corresponds to **A** sound the first letter. (who is) of universal presence and from the beginning.
The one who so understands.
all objectives attains. Indeed and the foremost he becomes.

9 When one chants AUM properly as taught by the Master, the **A** sound vibrates at the lower chakras, especially the mooladhara and the swadishthana.

This ensures optimal functioning of the senses and the intellect, thus one is able to perform well at work and at home.

Bit by bit one climbs the ladder and achieves success and fame. One delivers ever increasing targets and is able to touch international heights.

Verse 10 U-Dream = the Spark of Infinity

Dream state called Taijasa = the one with Spark corresponds to **U** sound the second letter. (which is) from improvement and double-edged gain. The one who so understands. he broadens the traditional knowledge base. And is a secular visionary. Indeed, among his descendants none is born ignorant.

10 At the heart center one experiences a fluid state that is not limited by the body or the mind. This state is the source of emotions and in this state one can go anywhere and experience anything.

No resource crunch, no relationship bitterness comes in the way. All goals seem puny, the one whom one wants comes straight to one's arms.

To the one who can dream, to him the pathways to greatness beckon.

When one chants AUM properly as taught by the Master, the **U**sound vibrates at the heart center. This frees up all knots and restores love, faith and innocence.

Verse 11 M-Sleep O I'm so Happy

Msound the third letter of AUM.
from discernment of the ultimate.
The one who so understands, He this all discerns. Indeed and becomes immortal.

11 When one's awareness rise to the higher chakras, at the third eye, then one is able to sift and discriminate. There is also the state of bliss at the sahasrara chakra, where one experiences deep rest.

One can then sense all the changing and also become aware of something that remains unchanged throughout.

This is the key to immortality.

When one chants AUM properly as taught by the Master, the **M**sound vibrates between the eyebrows and goes higher up as well. This frees up the *chitta* so that one can experience bliss, defenselessness, and eternity.

Verse 12 TURIYA TRANSCENDENTAL

the one who so understands, by the Self into the Self alone he merges.

12 Having known so many things of this world, having lived a full life and having had so many challenging adventures, one finally comes to the point of relaxation.
One understands that one knows not. There is an infinity to experience but it cannot be known or encapsulated within theories.

Having applied oneself thoroughly, having given 100% effort and shouldered all one's responsibilities, a time comes to drop it all.

Then one experiences the foundation state, the transcendental state that is ever present but hard to ascertain. This is called the TURIYA state in Vedantic lore. This is achieved only in deep meditation, in SAMADHI.

At the end, the state of deep stillness when one imbibes, one's soul merges into the cosmic soul.

This state dawns only for the wise, only for the one who has persevered patiently till the end.

END

5 The Mundaka Upanishad

Shanti Mantra

oṃ bhadraṃ karṇebhiḥ śṛṇuyāma devāḥ | bhadraṃ paśye
mākṣabhir yajatrāḥ | sthirairaṅgais tuṣṭuvāṃsastanūbhiḥ |
vyaśema devahitaṃ yadāyuḥ || svasti na indro vṛddhaśravāḥ
| svasti naḥ pūṣā viśvavedāḥ | svasti nastārkṣyo ariṣṭanemiḥ
| svasti no bṛhaspatirdadhātu || oṃ śāntiḥ śāntiḥ śāntiḥ ||

O Divine Wisdom!
May our ears listen to the sacred and the auspicious. May
our eyes see the propitious as we come together to partake
of wisdom.
May our limbs be firm and body attuned to long endurances.
May our senses function with full alertness and
May the sense of contentment be strong.
May our good thoughts form a discus to shield us and May
our education give us a shining personality.

Peace in our heart, in our body and in our environs.

Mundaka is from the Gopatha-Brahmana of the Atharva Veda. Whereas its Samhita portion survives in two recensions, after sages Paippalada and Shaunaka, the Brahmana portion available today is only of sage Gopatha. The Mandukya verses precede the Mundaka verses, which precede the Prashna verses in the Atharvaveda.

Mundaka Upanishad gets its name from "a head shaved of all heavy botherations", "an intellect clear of all doubts". By the sincere study of this Upanishad, one's mind resolves all troubles, difficulties seem trifles. It quenches the thirst of the sincere seeker and in beautiful verse satiates the heart of the ardent aspirant.

Mundaka is especially written for the man who is willing to rise above the crowd, whose performance in daily life is extraordinary, who is willing to work harder than his colleagues. It is for the soul who uses his talents to be creative and productive, and is at the same time thirsting for the Unknown.

muṇḍakopaniṣad - atha Muṇḍaka Upaniṣad

Now begins the Muṇḍaka

Upaniṣad means a deep connection with Divinity. The inward journey begins when one halts to probe. One merges the small mind into the BIG mind. One catches the wavelength of the Master.

Mundaka
= head shaved clean
= ego united with the supreme
= reasoning intellect freed of all doubt
= sensory mind freed from erroneous perception
= guilt washed away from the heart
= impressions rubbed out from the citta so that its
innocence is restored.

The Mysterious Karmic Plane

The human plane is designed to live a few lifetimes, say 400
years. Of course, with replacements of the anatomical body,
since that gets worn out by about 75 years. Those who play
the game well over the entire period, of 4 centuries, i.e. with
lots of cheerfulness and 100% effort, they automatically
attain Brahman. Souls that fail to appreciate the body-mind
complex and spend time in grumbling, complaining, back-
biting, or rather in being the frog in the well, get another 400
year span. This span is however with a handicap, in the
sense that the difficulties are formidable. This means that
those who are unlucky enough to repeat the cycle shall have
more moments of grief.

However the game ends after 800 years, all souls invariably
attain Brahman at the end.

Brahman is the plane of abundance, a plane where all souls
are fully nourished and satiated. Then by a desire to explore
other realms, some souls go to the karmic plane i.e., to our

plane of planet Earth. Other souls go to other realms, of that we shall talk about elsewhere.

1.1.1 A bit of tradition to create a soothing atmosphere for the great teaching to be delivered by means of a dialogue or satsang.

The eldest member of the family is called the Creator or Progenitor and also Protector or Nourisher. Creator since he is the first to build the home and furnish it with all necessities. Progenitor since he is the one who marries first and raises the family. Brahma is the generic term for grandpa.

We can also consider an inventor or entrepreneur or the one who started it as Brahma.

Brahma also means Protector. Obviously grandpa is the one who implemented whatever was needed for safety for his home, family and neighborhood. Grandpa ensured that his folks were well nurtured and his assets were properly cared for.

The Upanishad very intelligently begins with the word "Brahma" . This serves a number of objects. It is the reason why in the social & cultural traditions in every household, and in every institution the Founder is remembered, praised, and invoked. It helps children and youngsters to imbibe discipline and ingrain character and pragmatism.

Brahma is praised as the First among the Intelligent beings = homo sapiens. Brahma's birth is termed gratefulness for the birth of Intelligence. In any family, the brightest son or daughter is called, meaning the one whose birth makes the family (or an institute) exalted.

Now what did Grandpa do? He imparted the sum total of his life's experience, i.e. the complete knowledge of all subjects he was adept at, to his eldest progeny. Notice the placement of a very crucial word *atharvāya* = the one well versed in economic affairs, dutiful, hardworking, skilled, and upholding family name and tradition. In other words. Grandpa or the Founder of a Company, imparts key knowledge and painstakingly trains only the One who aptly qualifies for the position of successor. Continuing from previous verse, the next verse also adds color and atmosphere to the stage ambience by giving some background information.

1.1.2 Now this body of invaluable experiential wisdom first shared by Grandpa Brahma to his worthy successor Atharvan, was in turn added upon and disseminated. The worthy heir of yore propounded it to *aṅgiraḥ* i.e. to the select body of people or parliament or heads of staff.

Once we have a training methodology and the resources and tools for dissemination of our vision and mission, then we call all the officers of the company and brief them. This is how the system operates and it percolates down to the populace.

Then *satyavahaḥ* or the One who shares the whole truth without editing or abstracting, is adept at choosing the proper words, and has a flair for imparting; is selected to head *aṅgirasaḥ* i.e. the University (or Institution or Company or Nation).

Also, *satyavahaḥ* has the adjective *bhāradvājaḥ*, i.e.
endowed with speed, strength, integrity and tirelessness.
The word *aṅgirasaḥ* means a collection of Professors or
Masters or Sages who can take the vision forward in a very
holistic manner.

Guru is then the one to whom a big businessman or a big
leader or one who has seen enough of wealth and is
seeking liberation, approaches.

1.1.3 Shaunaka i.e., the one satiated with wealth and
thence turning to philosophy, goes seeking Angiras - the
Guru. On meeting the Guru, he pays due respects first by
serving the Guru, attending to his needs, i.e., seeing the
Guru is well-fed and well-clothed and well-rested.

Then Shaunaka poses the Mahavakya - the Ultimate
Question -

"O Dear Lord! What is it that being known, all this becomes
known?".
"O Dear Lord! What is it that being understood, life's puzzle
becomes clear?".

The devotee is asking how he may come to terms with life's
ups and downs. How may the storms of passion and the
vagaries of senses be cheerfully handled. How may the
mind be cleansed of doubt and the heart be rid of fear and
guilt? What is the way to unite with the Divine? What is the
key to Liberation?

or simply

How may he just do what he has set out to do?
(more or less on a regular basis!)

1.1.4 To him he thus replied, "The knowers of the Brahman or the enlightened Masters have spoken of two paths to liberation. **Para** = the path of gyana yoga, and **aPara** = the path of karma yoga. And both these paths are within each other, both these paths are to be followed simultaneously".

The Body needs a discipline of waking, eating, working, exercising, entertainment and rest. The mind needs a discipline of sadhana and satsang. Both are necessary. Both go together and are a perfect match.

Regularly one needs to visit Guruji and spend time in his satsang, meditation, discourse and seva. So also one needs to perform one's responsibilities and chores with honesty and dedication.

TIME-SPACE or BODY-MIND are a continuum. Name_&_Form or Sound_&_Light both make up this Duality and harmonizing both leads to Advaita.

Subject and Object, Emotions and Sensations, Theory and Practice, Phonons and Photons, Matter and Energy, both are to be well-understood and judiciously applied.

1.1.5 The Karma Yoga or *aparā vidyā* is fully detailed in the four Vedas, viz. Rigveda, Yajurveda, Samaveda, Atharvaveda; and the six Upavedas, viz. Shiksha, Kalpa,

Vyakarana, Nirukta, Chhandas and Jyotisha.

The Gyana Yoga or *parā vidyā* is the one by which Immortality is realized.

All of us go to school, then find work and raise a family. It is the process of Karma Yoga, doing what is right at that point in life, and moving forward. Simultaneously we seek to be at ease in the heart, resolving emotions, digesting thoughts, and keeping our innocence and purity intact. Initially when we are young, the Gyana Yoga is deeply ingrained and keeps working in parallel. As we get more colored or discolored by the vagaries of nature and society, the Gyana Yoga takes a back seat or is simply pushed under the carpet.

Then a day comes when Guruji (the Master or Divinity) comes in one's life. He lovingly takes one's hand and reestablishes one's balance. Then one can say Gyana Yoga has re-ignited.

This process may start at some definite point in life that is different for each one of us, and that is normal. Only the Seeker Finds. But what or who catalyzes one's seeking is hard to say. It is not written in any textbook nor taught in any school. That is what Angiras means when he says *atha parā yayā tad akṣaram adhigamyate.*

One may have started to balance Time and Resources, one's wealth might have shown a steady Climb, one's fame might have sky-rocketed,
BUT peace in the heart is another ball game!

Immortality does not mean gaining an imperishable body

or having immeasurable resources. Liberation does not mean living in a free country, getting desires fulfilled, or doing as one pleases. It cannot be succinctly put in words, but deep within, the heart knows it fully well. After all, it is in one's experience solidly as a baby or a youngster, then it starts to liquefy and by adult-hood it has become gaseous. Fitness is exactly what one is seeking, but until the time one stops, listens and asks the Guru, it is never addressed.

Like a sapling, the Guru's advice is also to be nurtured and assimilated bit by bit, so that faith and dispassion get firmly rooted within. Give it Time, give it Space, give it your very best shot.

Now the verse that gives the essence of Gyana Yoga and lays the foundation for stepping into the vast Unknown that is also known as Freedom.

1.1.6 Wisdom is not contained in the sensory perceptions.

Wisdom is something <u>different</u> from that
- which can be seen *adraiśyam*
- which can be grasped, handled or addressed *agrāhyam*
- which can be given any source attribute or genetic connotation *agotram*
- which has any flavor or shade or distinct feature *avarṇam*
- which has organs noticed in mammals *acakṣuḥśrotram apāṇipādaṃ* viz. eye ear hands feet, i.e. Wisdom is one that remains calm and at ease.

Wisdom is that which can be said
- to be continuous or eternal in Time *nityam*
- to be all that everyone perceives or realizes; or It is every

134 Mundaka

known and unknown object, whether living or dead,
whether animate or inanimate *vibhuṃ*
- to be present in everything or all-pervading in Space
sarvaga'taṃ
- to be Wonderfully sublime, fine yet beautiful, small yet
having a great impact *susūkṣmaṃ*
- to maintain Itself without any change *avyayaṃ* (due to
circumstance, natural phenomenon, person, place, time or
situation).

Wisdom is that which the brave and the intelligent
endowed with discrimination and detachment have, those
realized-Internally.

i.e.
There is no proof that Wisdom will show on anyone's
forehead or in his skin color or in his religious beliefs or in
his character or behavior or ...

i.e.
Saintliness is elusive both for the Subject and the Object. It
is an Internal or Hidden talent, and It has the capacity to
manifest in any being.

1.1.7 The Guru gives some practical examples to illustrate the point further.

> 1.7.1 As a spider weaves its web, and also swallows
> it from time to time
> 1.7.2 As deliciousNutritiousHealing herbs from the
> soil sprout
> 1.7.3 As on living men hair grow spontaneously on
> head and skin

1.7.4 Similarly it is all Happening in the world,
spiraling from the V A S T Infinite.

There is a logic somewhere, yet most of it is beyond logic.
Some things can be reasoned out, yet the majority is
beyond reason. Seemingly the plants and animals and
machines seem to have a fixed design, but the men who
create machines and nature that creates flora is
unpredictable.
Don't stop, Just Drop, and move on.

The Guru is giving an inkling of the Mahavakya "Verfiy some
facts, other facets simply accept with Faith, accept all
beings as your very own I Walk lightly as a cloud, be
humble as the grass.

And now the Master is indicating the means thereby.

1.1.8 Energy, Strength and Stamina are the result of

good discipline and long-term practice. Tapas is also
related to gainful employment since without that no divine
activity can be envisioned. Thereby skill is got and food can

be grown, eaten and digested.

With proper nutrition, the life force is sustained, the mind
and intellect function well, and Truth prevails in life i.e. in
the three worlds - inner heart, outer environment, close by
subtle currents.

Thence is derived the mastery over one's desires. Only
then can our expectations be properly met and our

aspirations fulfilled. This is called the Law of Karma or the cycle of human evolution.

$1.1.9$ The One who is omniscient all-knowing and has a deeper understanding of all laws. The One whose fire of discipline burns bright, whose lamp of wisdom is lit,

From that One – the Brahman, this big creation,
this V A S T nation, corporation, and galactic matter is produced and sustained.

Obviously to run a multi-billion-dollar empire a multi-faceted skill-set, enormous stamina, and an inventive mind are needed.

To rule over a nation, a high degree of resourcefulness, abundance of soft-skills and boundless energy are the key. Only then the cycle of peaceful growth and effervescent evolution are shaped.

Here ends the first part of the teaching. Close of the first semester of the first year of a three-year university degree program.

1st Year 2nd Semester

The student has survived the first term, in fact has done quite well, and is hopeful of finishing the first year on a high note.

The Master senses the enthusiasm and starts a new chapter of unlimited possibilities for the student.

Now begins the second part or the second semester.

The Master advises to refresh all that was taught earlier. Then he begins to talk on the practical aspects that will help in living to the best of one's abilities.

The principal topic is Praise for becoming rich and famous in the world, at the same time not let the heart be carried away and imprisoned by the entanglements and attractions.

Mundaka is highlighting the fate of the great souls. On one hand the famous can retain their goodwill and live till the end unstained and pure. On the other hand they can lose their balance and become embroiled in the storms of impure relationships and dealings.

The Laws of Motion

These are practical aspects of the laws of creation, also known as the plane of birth and death. This is the plane of human birth.

It is the karmic plane where the classical laws of Newtonian mechanics hold good:

1) Every object persists in its state of rest or uniform motion in a straight line unless it is compelled to change that state by an external force acting on it.
2) Force equals Mass times Acceleration.
3) For every action there is an equal and opposite reaction.

Restated

1) Law of Inertia
2) Law of Growth
3) Law of Conservation of Momentum

Later on, when the student clears the initial exams, the quantum mechanics and physics is explained, where respect rules, love is supreme.

1.2.1 This is the whole truth of the matter. This that has been taught in the last semester is the exact blueprint of life lived in the Treta - The age between 50 and 75 years when man is most experienced, broad-minded and useful to society at large.

Satyuga = Brahmacarya = Pure Childhood = 0 to 25.
Dvapar = Grihasta = all focus on earning = 25 to 50.
Treta = Vanprastha = endowed with viveka, vairagya, titiksha, uparati = 50 to 75 years.
Kalyuga = Sannyasa = again with a childlike mind but worn out body = 75 to 100 years.

Learn well and assimilate perfectly, so that you also walk the path as the heroes of yore. Just as the great men did it earlier, so shall you also live a life of beauty, charm, creativity, prosperity and happiness.

Learn from Virat Kohli, from Kane Williamson, from Jasprit Bumrah, from your chosen idol. Ingrain the teachings well. Go out and play, may your performance be splendid.

1.2.2 When nature is conducive, when the weather is bright and sunny, when the Gods are benevolent, when your mood is balanced, that is the time to reach out, work hard and go the extra mile.

Action is enjoined when the situation is ripe. In a Yagya, slowly stoke up the flames by pouring ghee in the correct space. That is an art. To maintain peak performance, lots of discipline and regular workouts are needed.

Do your efforts in tune to the need of the hour.

Time your strokes and stretches in accordance with the flexibility of your limbs. Make hay while the sun shines. Approach the administrator when his mood is conducive. Stock up in winter. Use an umbrella in the rainy season.

Now how to prevent a major fault, avoid unforced error, and not get into reckless living are taught.

1.2.3 Perform your task as advised and learnt, and be punctual and practice cleanliness. Only a few things can be done spontaneously, in the long run life should be lived with proper planning, mediation and preparation.

Some tasks need to be attended to daily, like our morning chores and rituals. Do not skip them.

Some tasks need to be carried out to the letter, strictly as per design, so do not miss any intermediate step. Like cooking or tea making or bank account opening or income tax filing, for such chores just follow the format without being too inventive.

Some tasks are fortnightly or monthly, like paying the bills,

getting the salary, going for a sauna or pancakarma, etc. no need to postpone or prepone these activities.

Some activities are dependent on the season like summer, monsoon, winter, so be not misaligned to that, rather be blessed that a change has come and cheerfully acknowledge the same.

Festivals and Celebrations and Birthday parties certainly cannot be given the cold-shoulder by not inviting guests and friends, or you shall find your relationships muddled and society shall look down upon you.

Be appropriate in attending to the needs of individual family members, and in dealing with various colleagues and staff and the boss at work. You must not behave in the same manner with the Guru as you behave with the devotees.

- in the army adhere to the military commandments, do not be official at home or vice versa.

Else your entire family and successors shall get tainted and suffer the backlash of faulty conduct.

1.2.4 Seven milestones in the human journey - birth, yagyopavit, university, marriage, job, raising a family, and liberation. Seven are the chakras from mooladhara to sahasrara. Seven seas and seven continents constitute the planet earth. Seven colors of the rainbow and seven notes in the musical octave and seven days of the week. In the Puranas, the Sun-God is described as riding a chariot drawn by seven horses.

Each milestone is likened to a bright flame that makes life go forward. Lighting the way and inspiring and propelling as well. Names of the milestone flames have been given to add grace, lend charm and be easily memorized. Just as in school so many rote items are given a catchy phrase.

fragrant sense alluring, lines on the palm = design template, fast as the mind; deep red – enthusiastic; deep gray – serious; dancing figure, dazzling, the most beautiful consort of Creation.

1.2.5 To the one who is regular in performance of duty, honest and earnest and gives painstaking attention to every detail; such a one easily climbs the ladder to the top. His merit is amply rewarded, there is phenomenal increase in his responsibilities, and he quickly ascends to the highest post.

1.2.6 Success beckons, fame nudges, society kisses, divinity takes him by the hand. He is given a red-carpet welcome wherever he goes, and accorded a high seat of honor.

1.2.7 These eighteen virtues, tools or skills are highly prized by the lay public, particularly by the media, also known as the fourth estate.

However it is not enough to rise outwardly. If the inner Being is not listened to or properly addressed, then name and fame and wealth and glory come to naught. Their transient nature gets revealed soon enough. One must not get stuck in the outer.

One must never stop toiling even after attaining purity of thought. One must not give up humility, punctuality, innocence and belongingness.

The ego of righteousness, or the ego of a successful man is a dangerous pitfall. Such an ego can destroy all merit in the twinkling of an eye.

1.2.8 Like the blind led by the blind, a scientist or professor or infatuated artist or high official or successful businessman can succumb to this dangerous ego and get trapped. His evolution then stops, and his decline begins.

His foolish company might keep him in raptures of delight, but there are wicked storms waiting to cause his ruin by and by.

Peace in the heart and clarity in the mind are adversely affected by fame and wealth - this golden principle is stated boldly.

1.2.9 Ignorance stalks those riding the foolish winds of worldly glory. Ignorance gnaws at the heart and shrouds all wisdom.

The wheel turns full circle and one is thrown to the bottom of the ladder again. This is a big mystery, and bigger still is that so many popular people bite the dust in the end.

Then there is no way out, since
- the body has lost its youthful charm,
- the mind has lost its suppleness, and
- the intellect no longer knows how to surrender, being shackled by dizzying memories.

1.2.10 Bodily illness and emotional friction in relationships makes their life miserable in old age, the years from 75 to 100 are also called Kalyuga.

Based on intellectual deeds devoid of divine vision, in old age they may lead a life not wishing for anything better, or even be subject to a clueless survival.

An important point.
The Upanishad is not talking about fantasy, dream, or improbable after life goodies. It is boldly stating the practical, here and now in this lifetime.

<u>Babyhood to OldAge alone is outlined</u>.
(some commentators interpret it as after life, no matter since it is well within the 400-year span).

1.2.11 On the other hand Sannyasa in that age is the golden time that comes to those engaged in tapas, austerity, surrender and devotion.

Maintain these simple living traits even after having reached the pinnacle, since then alone can the body and mind be safe-guarded in old age. And the heart kept blemish free.

Fear and worry cannot touch such souls. Illness too has no

wickedness for them. Their life in old age is a harmony, being cleansed of all attachments, it is as if illumined by the gentle light of the sun.

If your old age is peaceful and filled with cheerful love and devotion, that is the highest attainment. This is stated as immortality in the scriptures.

1.2.12 O Seeker! if thou art smart, if thou art intelligent, then in youth itself thou shalt take refuge in the Master.

In the prime of life you shall make it a priority to reach out to Guruji.

You shall not defer it till later. You shall seek the company and counsel of Wisdom. You shall attend satsang and become regular in sadhana and spiritual practices.

Yoga and Meditation shall form a tamper-proof part of your daily rituals. You shall serve the Master with a pure heart till the end.

1.2.13

For such a soul is the veil of ignorance shattered. To him the Guru himself reveals the fount of wisdom. The divine makes the meeting certain. The highest knowledge is then imparted by the preceptor to the disciple. Qualifications of the seeker are clearly stated.

1) Non-arguing intellect. An employee or student or servant fits the bill when his nature is humble, ready to listen, willing to accept.
2) Having balance in lifestyle. The student who is willing to work indoors as well as outdoors, who

gives time to family, hobby, meditation, who has a discipline in eating and spending.

Method of Instruction is given clearly.
1) In great detail. Comprehensive and exhaustive treatment of the subject. Proper, complete, and fulfilling lectures.
2) In practical form. The highest skill cannot be imparted without real-life training. Hands-on projects, industry internships, and enough practice makes the man perfect.

2nd Year 1st Semester

Strangers, acquaintances, distant cousins, foreigners cannot go to those depths of nadir, since they have no emotion to drive it.

Conversely the charm of togetherness and beauty of bonding between two people is what Sparks off the greatest inventions, discoveries, entrepreneurships and enduring tales of mankind.

A wonderful story hinges on a superb cast. A great institution is forged by the teamwork of family members and partners.

This verse boldly says that all humans have much in common; and that can serve as an antidote and heal many relationships. Similarly it points to the undeniable fact that in the process of manufacturing (or birth) we unavoidably imbibe some distinct traits, which again is good for us. Then it goes on to mention the sameness of our death and departure. We all discard the body.

2.1.1 Everything is born from the One. From one sun countless rays reach every nook and corner of our planet. From the fire in our hearth brilliant sparks keep us warm as those from the *Lohri* bonfire. All of us drink water from the regular rains, from oceans, lakes and rivers. And we all breathe the same oxygen and eat the grain grown by the same farmer.

An entire village gets populated from the union of a couple.

Now why is this verse so important? What is it trying to convey? And how does that help in our daily life?

Firstly it tells us to strongly etch the fact that we are all from the same stock. We are all made up of the same thing. We all have the same core, the disparity is superficial.

This fact is a big relief. This idea is a great leveler of ego. It can erase bitterness and make us equanimous, productive, and creative on a large scale that is the result of strong teamwork.

This verse also highlights another poignant reality. Maximum hate, conflict and destruction can only occur between family members - Father and Son, Brother and Brother. Or between two married people or between close friends.

2.1.2 Brahman is thought of as

luminous, formless, all pervading, unborn, benevolent, not requiring sustenance, not requiring decision making, from the eternal, beyond all lofty imagination.

The imagination of the seer stretches far. The divine is honored in the most exalted ways. The sky's the limit. To achieve anything grand, aim for the stars.

Goodness has no parallel. It has no compromises. No adjustments, shortcuts, half-hearted attempts. No rush, no hurry, no tension.

There is an abundance. It is enough. All can be taken care of. None is left un-provided for. Nothing comes in the way. No hurdles, jams, nor any conflicts.

2.1.3 From the majestic effulgent Being,

the conscious life force,
the reasoning faculty,
all senses and organs,
the vast empty spaces so essential for growth,
the nourishing air,
the light and fire,
the water and fluids, and
the divine mother Earth that contains and sustains all beings and things

is manufactured.

2.1.4 And of the Divine we can visualize
- fire as the forehead for crystal clear thinking
- moon and sun as the eyes that see in night as well as day, the eyes that observe everything since they do not shut nor rest

- the four quarters as the ears that hear every little tremor, shake, and pin drop
- diverse scriptures, textbooks, and methods of schooling and instruction as speech
- interstellar space and air as the throbbing life-force,
- the universe with ceaseless activity as its pulsating heart
- this planet Earth its domain of target setting and goal attaining – a step forward.

The Brahman is the innermost soul of every being. He is contained in the sinner and the saint. He is in the flower and the paint.

2.1.5 The cycle of procreation proceeds from

- Fire that ignites passion and like the Sun makes fusion possible
- Clouds that bring rain and cause food to grow
- Moon that infuses vitality into herbs in the soil
- The Male who is thus well nourished by the food becomes empowered to make the female pregnant.

Many such occasions cause multiple births to happen. All types of flora, fauna and beings are thus created.

2.1.6 From Brahman emerge the energies - Rik that manifests cosmic laws, Sama that balances, Yajus that formulates individual emotions and thought processes.

From Brahman emerges the special faculty of training, imparting skill, and education, especially from parents to children for all mammals.

From Brahman the systems of manufacturing and gainful employment. Thereby the merits and earnings.

Due to Brahman the yearly cycle of time comes into existence.

Due to Brahman some assume authority and status and can thus govern and conduct affairs.

Due to Brahman the galaxies got formed.

And to Brahman's credit the all fulfilling, purifying, and blessing nature of the moon and the sun that shine on all.

2.1.7 Due to Brahman's will manifested gods with varying talents, the enlightened masters, the common folks, animals and birds.

Brahman willed the involuntary functions like respiration and excretion.

Brahman then created all grains and delicacies.

Brahman advocated the spiritual practices of rigorous discipline, staunch faith, truthfulness, balance in action and inaction, and social laws.

2.1.8 Seven is his magical figure. He made
- 7 pranayama – nadi shodhana, ujjayi, bhastrika, kapalbhati, bhramari, agnisara, sudarshan kriya
- 7 light colors –vibgyor - rainbow

- 7 service acts needed by every household – cooking, cleaning, washing, gardening, carpentry, plumbing, electricals
- 7 types of earning activity - farming, mining, manufacturing, processing, trading, publishing, counseling
- 7 continents/seas/planets
- 7 chakras, the major energy centers - mooladhara to sahasrara

7 deep seated virtues are his signature or presence.

See Patanjali Yoga Sutras – a) Friendship, b) Kindness, c) Cheerfulness, d) Absence of fear, e) Absence of obsession, f) Clarity of mind, and g) Pragmatic vision.

2.1.9 So also from him the calm oceans and majestic mountains manifest. And water bodies of varied hue, blue lakes, gurgling streams, roaring rivers.

By his will nutritious vegetables and juicy fruits, all sensuous pleasures.

And in the midst of all this splendid distraction,
he ensconces himself, placid-pure-innocent.

2.1.10 Both flavors, The paths of Karma Yoga and of Gyana Yoga, find his favor and his complete approval.

The soul that glimpses this truth, lives life with such clarity of vision in total acceptance, that soul triumphs, sheds the knotty fricative ignorance in this life itself, and attains Nirvana.

O beloved seeker! Own this teaching and you also become immortal.

Here ends the first term of the second year on a promising note.

2nd Year 2nd Semester

the name, luminous, firmly fixed foundation fluidly circulating in the heart cavity - herein this big universe centered is.
that moves, breathes, winks and this that is beyond the real and imaginary, beyond logic, that ultimate wish of all beings you perfectly welll recognize.

2.2.1 It is effulgent, near at hand and ready to help, giving many glimpses and nudges, but packaged in
the ordinary easy to miss moments.

So a silent stable mind is required to sense it moving in a heart that is filled with love. A breath that is quiver free makes it possible.

The supreme prize is he, he is the one worth seeking. He is the fountain of joy and one's firm foundation.

He is both the dance and the dance floor for whatever that moves, breathes, or blinks.
Grasp this essential truth with an open mind.
He is All that is eternal and also all that is transient.
He is all that is desirable, attractive and luxurious.
He is top-seeded, topmost, the VVIP.

152 Mundaka

And he is too big to be cognized by the mind, imagined by the heart, or contained in any brainwave.

2.2.2 That which glows brilliantly and is hence visible to all,

That which is subtler than the finest particle and hence can escape being noticed by the best of scientists,
That in which all galaxies and black holes are contained,

That in which all thoughts, fantasies, emotions and sensations, desires, expectations and aspirations are clearly experienced,
That is This.
Named the immutable Brahman.
He is the life story of all beings.
It is the sound emerging from every lip.
It is the cause of every reason or decision.
That is the Truth.
That is the sweetest delight.
By the full force of the mind and all faculties, Seek, Respect, Understand and Assimilate.

O Worthy Aspirant! That Brahman you must get schooled in.
Make that your Priority, Focus, Goal.

2.2.3 By the practice of Upanishad, sitting close, available, all ears,

String your bow of deep adoration, honor and reverence.

Fix on it the arrow of your senses with laser like sharpness, your mind immersed in meditative contemplation, your body thoroughly loose and relaxed.

Thus taking aim at the clear target that shows itself in the tranquil heart, loosen your arrow within, enter that Divine space with good cheer.

Become one and United with that.

Fuse, melt, dissolve, lose yourself in that infinite peace.

Now the means of practice, the steps of Sadhana

2.2.4 The chant of Om

 forms a great sound envelope that equips the mind with resourcefulness, as the twang of a great bow heralds victory.

The Soul united with the body, the senses, the intellect, the citta and the ego becomes a yogic arrow that speeds unerringly towards its aim.

The target is only that one God, also known as Brahman, Shiva, Tao and by other diverse names.

or

You may call it Love, Kindness, Purity.

Use your entire will, attention, intention, and sincere earnestness to attain the Lord and merge with him.

Let Brahman be your prime passion and ultimate reward.

Make all your activities resound with his name, also called Om.

Certainly this birth is precious and in this very body justify it by living a yogic life and attain Oneness with the Supreme.

2.2.5 Another thing that shall greatly help your Sadhana is to mind your tongue from uttering anything casual, frivolous, grumbling or hurtful.

Stop loose talk forthwith.

Refrain from hurting anyone through your tongue.

Then instantly you shall realize that all that you see –
- bodies, objects, flora and fauna; and
- all that you interact with - land, space, and atmosphere; and also
- all that you experience within - breath, mind, heart, and the rest

It is all tightly interwoven in the Brahman, nay it is all composed of Brahman alone.

The moment you get such a glimpse; know that you are well on track, your aim is soon achieved,
Nirvana awaits you.

2.2.6 Your navel center is the hub on which all nerves connect like the spokes on the wheel of life.

Deep inside your heart is the space where Brahman resides and rules your world by twitching the nerves, throttling some, loosening others.

Everywhere it is the same, each particle, ant, virus or human, is so impregnated and ruled by Brahman.

And particularly in this human body - sense him, identify with the inner conscience, and befriend him by means of the sacred syllable Om.

Meditate on Brahman by chanting Om.

That shall surely make the task of crossing the dangerous river of inky darkness unscathed.

You shall certainly pass from this world guilt free, blame free, Free.

Gurudev advises to suffix Om with a mahavakya e.g.
Om Namah Shivaya,
Om Namo Bhagavate Vasudevaya
Om Tat Sat, etc.

who is all knowledgeable and all perceiving, whose glory on this earth is. in the luminous township of infinity verily this is, in inner space the soul is comfortably seated. The one conditioned by thoughts, the owner of life-force and body, is firmly placed in the nourishing food, in the close vicinity of the heart. it by scientific vision fully realize the Brave ones, its joyful nature, its strengthening nectar is what illumines all.

2.2.7 The great men and women make life worth living by setting an example. Their life has all the flavors and pitfalls that come to you as well, yet they live with a graceful charm.

The Brahman is awakened in them, or we can say Brahman

owns their body, Brahman rules their mind, Brahman guides them in all transactions, and Brahman is all they care for.

They are discriminating and particular about their habits, food, lifestyle and sangat. They are careful whose company they choose and whom they avoid.

This helps them sail smoothly in life. This sets them apart from the rest. This gets them the epithet - the bold, the beautiful, the successful brave.

If you ask them - have you seen God? Their reply is almost always –
- God is the only light my eyes see,
- God alone is he who comes to mind,
- God colors my thoughts, and
- God rules my emotions.

2.2.8 Pure becomes the heart in their company. Doubts vanish, guilt melts, impressions and karma get burnt.

Such is the blazing company of the wise. That is what an enlightened master does.

The Guru resolves all conflicts, cures all ills, he brings you home to Oneness.

This happens in those who are able to see that **Opposite values are complementary in nature.**

Those who can sense the Divine's hand in ups and downs, in fluctuating seasons, joys and frustrations.

Who never ever lay the blame on anyone, who do not nourish guilt, nor harbor doubt.

2.2.9 You become golden. You become luminous. You sparkle and shine, your light reaches far and wide.

Your purity speaks for itself, your divinity is your ticket.

You are hailed as a knower of Brahman. You become a realized soul.

The Brahman is eulogized. The Saint is praised.

It is very hard to attain sainthood. It is most difficult to become pure. It needs lots of patient practice to achieve a level where you become the lighthouse to guide many on the path.

This can only be appreciated by those at the top. Those who made it through.

Only an able mother knows how much effort is needed to raise good children. Only the housewife knows how much time and energy is required to cook something lip-smacking delicious and nutritious to boot!

A famous and oft quoted verse from the Upanishads.

there sunlight not illumines, nor moonlight nor starlight,

these lightning flashes do not reveal,
how then this flame?

that alone is shining,

by its light all this reflects, all of this illumines

158 Mundaka

$2.2.10$ There no sensory light reaches, that is fathomless, silent and still.

There is no distinction there, no features of any sort even when examined under the blazing sun or the cool moonlight or even the faintest star. Purity is a seamless whole, that the light of intellect does not grasp, nor does lightening illumine.

Then how could our small candle flames or fancy torches or puny ego reach there?

By Brahman is the functioning of men and machines, By it is governed the tempest and the breeze.

All is made brilliant by its kindly light, all of us touch glory under its shade.
Any victory or fame is due to its grace. Any win is its will. All powerhouses are powered by it,
Man becomes a king or saint due to its kindness.

$2.2.11$ Mate - all of this, that, it, you and me are the living examples of that immortal Brahman.

Brahman is in Front, it is behind, to the left and to the right, my dear in the center of everything too. Up above in the heavens is Brahman, down below in hell as well.

The past was Divine, the future shall be Divine,
Wake up and see, the present too is perfect!

Whether you do right or you sense wrong, whether it is the

past history or the future in the making, it is all willed, supervised, ordered and witnessed by Brahman.

Let go of your obsession, loosen your scruffiness, and wipe out your ill-will, Love alone rules, nay Light alone is this magnificent universe.

Here ends the second year, filling the mind with awe, clearing all the doubts, and establishing firm faith in the good.

3rd Year 1st Semester

Life's last term doesn't ever end! It spills into the daily grind, it fashions the future.

Story Time

Now comes the story time. The best orator, the acclaimed speaker, the famous school; all give due attention to anecdote, entertainment, live examples, practical wisdom.

Story time. Lighten up fellas. Relax. Just sit back and enjoy the ride.

3.1.1 Nara and Narayana

Have you seen a tree teeming with birds and bees? Have you spent any time tiptoeing in the woods? Have you seen the stunning sunset? Or had pets and fishes and friends?

What do you notice? What does the intellect see?

It is the same tree or school or workplace or village. The sounds and delights and ambience is the same for all.

Yet is each animal the same? Is each sibling satisfied with the same toy?

One is quiet, reserved, content and shy. The other is gregarious, outgoing, social and ambitious.

One sits calm, amused and nondescript, the other aggressively pursues attention, cash backs and rewards.

3.1.2 And what happens after a while my friend?

After a life of toils and travails, having spent all energy running hither tither, having attained great rewards yet not the one that satiated the soul,

perchance one spots the wise in the vicinity.

One's inward eye is opened and one sees the calm co-traveller. The saint so near and accessible, a sight for sore eyes, and soothing like some heavenly balm.

One begins to experience Grace, one opens up to the ultimate embrace.

3.1.3 We all seek inspiration. In the smallest trifling matter, we are looking for excitement, reward or appreciation.

Lo and behold, what then if Lord himself grants a vision. One look of his, one glimpse of Bliss, one experience of the highest, and then our life changes entirely.

No more then doth the mind crave after puny deprivations. No thought thence chases rotten pathways, nor does tongue get taste from druggy culture or kick from smoky sensations.

Lust gets erased from the heart, the knot of begging society for imagined or material gains loosens up.

Imperishable habits face instant closure, tendency to invite illness, destruction, shame loses steam.

Self-cheating and self-denial rupture apart; guilt, fear, blame and associated stains imposed on self and on society fade.

A human life is born.

3.1.4 Human birth is indeed fragile, human birth is not of the body nor has anything to do with the physical.

In the famous American visa application they verify wealth - just how short-sighted can they get! And to verifying goodness they don't even try.

In some big muscular corporations they seek others extinction, sadly the plot has cast them using demonic neurons.

Well but what of the energy that courses through them, and what of the emotions that heave in my bosom? The wise declare it all is Brahman....

Soon you laugh, you split, you break up. Soon you embrace the Divine and acknowledge its dark shades. Soon it hits home that America and Afghanistan are both A grade and both are Brahman.

Sometimes you play the part of the hero, and sometimes of the heroine, both are one and the same Brahman. Only when the shaft hits bull's eye, only when the center is pierced, only when respect reverence and awe take charge of life Irrespective of news, views, analysis and observation, does enlightenment dawn. Such is the mysterious majestic life of the knowers of the Brahman.

3.1.5 When both pain and pleasure are Brahman, when any trade practice, law or system has equal rating, what does one choose?

Up to you is easily said, but the brave wishes for courage, patience, kindness and discipline.

When white is pure and so is black and so also the whole gamut of intervening hues, can't one take any shade and go forward?

Trick question mate. Don't let it fool you.

When everyone is reveling in smoke and drink shouldn't you too take a bite? That is just sowing the seeds of a bitterly painful pitfall that will manifest after such a long time that you and your succeeding generation can never connect, and simply traverse the same destructive and unfulfilling trail again!

So much for theory, the story has become rather tacky.

Please clear this puzzling painting called Brahman.

The wise declare with all humility - yes all paths lead to Rome, any trick will get you there, eating sleeping entertaining and the short-lived thing called working are designed for each soul.

But if you are smart, if you are intelligent, if you are seeking only the very best, then you shall with conscious effort embark on strengthening the core values common to all cultures and civilizations.

Friendliness, kindness, gentleness, caring, and sharing. You shall never then be tempted to fall prey to speaking ill. You shall be most careful to keep a strict watch on your tongue. You shall then never slander, abuse or spread gossip. You shall spend more and more time in a spiritual context,

That delights all, hurts few and radiates a deep sense of love, peace, and good-will.

This they declare as the sweetest path, filled with purifying grace.

3.1.6 Truth Triumphs.

What of falsehood? Falsehood appears to win initially. Since both are inherent in Brahman, both seem to be victorious, albeit in different situations, at different times, or for different people.

Yet when wisdom dawns in life, one always takes the path of truth, one is not tempted by untruth.

Isn't this a bit muddy or tangential? Not at all, once you start tasting the rewards of truthfulness, the brave declare, you shall never ever be foiled by untruth. The path of truth takes a while to come into focus and it is the direct path to Brahman.

Untruth seems easy, attractive, and tempting, but after a long long time, it gets you thoroughly imprisoned, you fall terribly ill, and eke out a miserable existence. No doubt you reach Brahman, but such a path is not recommended.

In the end only the Truth wins. There is no contest, the honest win hands down.

3.1.7 Since the path of righteousness is fraught with grave danger initially, no one understands or seeks it.

Since possibilities are immense, since opinions vary, since diverse schools propound contradictory tenets, it cannot be grasped by the faint- hearted.

The one without intense determination cannot unravel the complex equations leading to Brahman.

The lazy lethargic dull-headed is soon lost and mired in the maze of Brahman's staggering tempestuous networks, the weaklings get lured by its myriad dazzling lights and end up in a heap by the wayside.

For the one who never chooses to practice purity, the nondescript Brahman remains elusive till the very end.

He keeps searching for that one drop of nectar, he keeps

begging to get his illness cured, but Brahman remains hidden. For he has never sought to open his own heart. He has never allowed grace to enter his dense brain.

3.1.8 Why is it that it is forsaken by some stupid yet wealthy? Why is it that those whom the media chooses to highlight regularly get caught in material density?

Friend - our senses are not equipped to acknowledge it. Logic and reason fall flat trying to grapple with it. The fourth estate invests a lot on stories based on deception, greed, aggression or fanaticism, and the social media goes viral only when they spot someone's lame mistake. Remember all of this is few and far between, these are worst case examples that just happen. The majority is far unconnected, a wonder it pays willingly to read the stories!

How can those who hunger for outside news ever realize what's cooking within? When all the antennae are pointed outwards to snoop on unlucky neighbors, the space inside remains void and null. It cannot attain, nor can it welcome.

So friend only when you focus earnestly on Brahman, only when you reach out to Him, only when you Meditate and step within, can you glimpse love, can you taste Bliss, can you get established in secure wisdom.

3.1.9 With regular sadhana, and Guruji's hollow and empty advance meditation courses, the workings of the vital life-force and its constituents - the 5 airs, viz. prana, apana, vyana, udana and samana get slowly revealed.

The para-sympathetic yogic practices that cause stress to be balanced in contrast with the sympathetic stress elevating systems of gymming and aerobics, also reveal the brain wave frequency spectrum to be composed of alpha, beta, gamma, Delta and Theta.

As this knowledge filters in, the 5 components of consciousness also become distinctly clear - sensuous mind, intellect, memory, ego and soul.

Then one's practices take a new turn of sincerity, regularity and priority. Thereby the heavy veil of ignorance gets worn and translucent, and the self-shines forth brightly.

This is known as direct experience of the pure soul.

3.1.10 The saint endowed with such discrimination and soaked in the purity of dispassion, gets the upper hand on nature's energies. Its forces are then ever at his beck and call.

The physical laws bend to his wishes automatically, the primordial energies succumb to his laser-like mind that is free of conflict.

Hence anyone desirous of success must approach a Master with all humility and serve him, thereby ensuring self-growth, evolution and freedom.

Thus ends the 5th semester or the 1st part of the 3rd year, where the disciple learns the tools of the trade and gets to practice dispassion and meditation, and his faith is strengthened.

The Final Term

The living plane is sinusoidal in design. Also known as the karmic roller coaster. It is all relative or tangential here. Actually, none is good, nothing and no one is bad. It is just a play of Divine and demonic energies, as we experience in the Hari Om Meditation. The Sanskrit word captures the essence far better, sur/asur without causing fear, turmoil, aggression. English being in its infancy, is still struggling to say things as they are, without adding the polarity, shade or spice of the reporter.

Some thrive on the crest, others like the trough, few balance in the middle.

After a while of resting and replenishing the thrill of excitement grips Brahman, some Sparks burst forth and escaping from its gravity, take birth in the sinusoidal plane - known by many names, the Relative, the Dvaita, the Leela, the Karmic.

It is rather a new beginning for all who land up here in the karmic. At the start of the 400 years lifespan, as children we are all the same, only the surrounding culture and societal fabric vary.

Freedom

The Guru has implicit faith in Brahman. He knows this is Brahman's play, direction, law and governance.

The realized soul lives in total acceptance. It is an acceptance that is un-tamperable. When the intellect has become soft like butter, and regular Sadhana keeps the citta free of troublesome memories, then a moment dawns when nature's energies, physical laws, and man-made events lose all potential in his presence. In other words the forces become calm, placid, and undisturbing for him.

That is the reason the Guru moves free. He does not despise anyone. He has no fear of natural calamity. He has not an iota of doubt.

The Guru's focus and determination are so strong and his identification with Brahman so total that he begins to consider all as holy and sacred. He reveres all, denies none.

This makes his aura luminous and it resonates far and wide. Humans, animals, trees, and rivers become his friends. Seasons are easy on him, illness too doesn't bother much.

This is the story of Nirvana, freedom.

3.2.1 This is the means to attain enlightenment.

Those brave souls who take the path of regularity in Sadhana, Satsang, Silence and proper diet, become bereft of superfluous needs and wants.

Moods and emotions become benevolent, desires become trifles.

In time their steadfastness attains the point of total power matching. After they have made their mark in the world, after they have balanced the forces of good and evil, they journey forth to the plane free of old age, sickness, lack.

They simply ascend the ramp since their aura matches its potential. That plane is also called the plane of absolute Brahman.

3.2.2 In case we have changed the body within the 400 year span, then as children we shall be born with some genetic traits from the previous lifetimes. These so called karmic impressions will make us susceptible to behave and speak and act in a specific manner when faced with a person or situation.

However this is only a probability, determined by how strong the impressions are and how big a challenge the current moment poses. In case we get lucky to come to Guruji with an open mind, then his teachings, especially the Sudarshan Kriya, will just erase those impressions, or make them quite faint in the very least. Then the journey of the remaining 400 years will not only become delightful, productive, and graceful, it shall also rub off on those we interact with and make their flight smooth.

Such souls then may go back to the source or plane of Bliss sooner than 400 years, or wish to play longer and retire only at the end of 400 years.

In any case, even those who fail to adopt a value system or ingrain some healthy discipline, attain Brahman at the end of 400 years. Only their total lifespan shall have a lot of grief and suffering, too much turmoil, blemish or shame. Not to worry, since some souls have been seen to have such proclivity, As you sow so shall you reap.

3.2.3 A big bouncer is hurled at so called fanatics who lean to extreme righteousness or strict religiousness or other harsh Puritan measures.

This Brahman does not favor lengthy discourses, it does not filter into cutting edge intellect, crazy genius, or prodigal sons. It is not revealed by rote learning of any text, philosophy, or methodology.

Only the brave soul willing to take responsibility with a cheerful heart and Open mind is whom Brahman favors.

The key is discipline with a joyful acceptance of every experience and an openness that keeps the mind flexible for Brahman's entry.

Evenness of temper, tranquility of emotion, a heart free of rigid obsessiveness, these are the qualities Brahman manifests in.

Fitness of both mind and body, pleasant countenance, balance in diet and exercise, refraining from harsh, bitter, or mocking speech, such aspects are most conducive for Brahman's welcome.

3.2.4 Most theories emphasize mental clarity and skillset, however that additionally needs a supple mind, a strong frame, and a loving heart, to qualify for Brahman.

When we see a healthy baby, we feel overjoyed. When we see a robust personality, it evokes confidence. A fit body has perhaps been overlooked by some theoretical physicists and armchair orators, so the Master quells it.

Another point to beware of is logic in excess or profane logic or illogical reasoning. Such a mindset has firmly shut the doors to Brahman.

Also body torture, unpleasant antics, destructive rituals lead one nowhere. Any practice that is only slanted to draw attention or create commotion is far removed from Brahman.

At the same time the ordinary man who does not gossip, refrains from rumor mongering, pursues his own honest duty, and maintains his civility and gentleness, gets easy access to Brahman.

3.2.5 Sages who find resonance with Brahman attain samadhana, a deep contentment. Gratefulness becomes evident in their behavior, and serenity reflects on their face.

Likes and dislikes no longer categorize them, affability and grace exude from them.

These Yogis, brave adventurers committed to the truth, their every cell infused with strong faith, their entire being brimming with Divine embrace, Own the great Brahman with open arms, and immerse themselves fully in the Oneness.

This is an experience par excellence, this is a journey beyond rewards, this is what the pure heart longs for, this is the fondest dream.

3.2.6 The greatest adventurers, the brilliant entrepreneurs, the artists deeply connected to their art, the cheerful sportsmen, happy-go-lucky school children, doting mothers and the perfect yogis, they all have the stamp of Brahman.

They all thrive in Brahman, and with joyful harmony live their lives.

Folk around them sense the soothing aura they radiate, all feel blessed in their presence. Many claim they help fulfill aspirations, wishes, dreams! Why not, when you feel good, certainly your performance raises and your efforts fructify.

Their dropping of the body is so calm and peaceful, their onwards journey is marked with happy composure, the whole world celebrates their liberation.

3.2.7 The 5 senses, 5 organs of action, and the 5 objects to which the senses get drawn, i.e. the 5 elements - Earth, water, air, light and space, these 15 gross constituents of the body-mind complex get freed from their moorings at the time of passing of the soul from the karmic plane to the blissful plane.

Before the end of the 400 year average timespan, they dissolve in Brahman since no impressions remain for a new body to clothe the soul. (Of course their will to play further and be reborn is always granted if that be the case).

The subtle body responsible for the functions
  - of the central nervous system,
  - the autonomous respiration, etc.,

- the luminous thought and emotion generating mechanisms,
- citta and ego sacs,

all of these subtle energies also bid adieu from the brave soul.

That soul is then ideally pure and without any cover or color, so its merger with Brahman is total and indistinguishable.

3.2.8 Even as springs and tributaries and rivers race gleefully to unite with the ocean where their limited identifications are all erased and the union is total,

And no more inside the ocean can anyone then name the original streams, nor sense the original color, flavor, or taste,

So also do the liberated souls get united with Brahman. **(Please do not forget that all of us too eventually do the same).** The words - liberated, brave, saintly etc., simply refer to their existence when alive in body as joyous, free, pure. Compared to that the existence of the common populace has a two-fold difference.

1. The highs and lows are intense and create much heat, friction, and strong impression. The overall quality of life is poor, shoddy, unenviable.
2. For sure the ride shall span 400 years, in extreme cases 800. And that too just imagine - filled with pain, misery, illness, crashed relationships, a fearful horror show.

A question may be asked - if the soul remains impure at the end of 400 years how can it merge with Brahman? Mate - it is due to the time principle.

All of us who do Nadi Shodana Pranayama, have heard the instruction - 9 rounds or 5 minutes at least. In plain words the Pranayama ends in 5 minutes, whether you do it correctly or incorrectly.

That is Brahman's working, after a certain time everything dissolves, the movie ends, all actors retire backstage.

A new script is then enacted from scratch. In it the previous villain might play the hero, the earlier heroine might be some hapless maid.

The river example includes pure waters, sullen tributaries, muddy streams, dangerous gorges, foul drains, placid seas.

3.2.9 A soul that attains Brahman well in time is highly regarded. His stories are sung, his exploits become legendary, books are filled with his glory.

Many philosophies are propounded concerning him, many people seek to emulate him. Many assume his ownership, many claim him ancestor.

The one amongst us who reaches Brahman first is treated as God. That is why God is worshipped in so many names and forms all over the world. That one Brahman is mistaken to have a particular body, race, religion or set of attributes.

A hero is honored by some, others laud someone else, possibly many are unaware of the two!

Brahman is difficult to typify, it doesn't fully fit any known person, entity or idol, yet it is definitely all. All are his subsets, all attributes are his.

Many unknown unsung heroes, saints, divine souls roam the planet. Their chief quality is a loving, accepting, large heart.

One may become quite balanced and pragmatic in day to day living, but one is really tested in the extreme circumstances.

The one who allows the wickedest event to pass without causing bitter impression, nay who offers his profuse thanks to the almighty that he was chosen for the cruel storm, he alone is said to have untied all the knots in the heart. He alone has become soft as Brahman while still in body.

This stage is referred to as the immortal existence.

Immortality refers to the fact you are no longer trying to duck, prevent, escape or be in any sort of blockage or denial.

3.2.10 Clean Shaven, head Shaven too. Mundaka. The monk with clarity of vision, no cloudiness. The man with nothing to hide in his beard. The soul with an ego that is light, a memory that is untainted. A Shave, as in handsome, shining, clean, pure. Innocent as a New born.

That is why our Advance Meditation Course AMC is called a journey - From the Head to the Heart.

A soul who is committed to AMC with a yogic attitude, with fairness and non-prejudice, easily shakes off all burdens of the head, becomes a Mundaka.

This Upanishad makes sense to such a soul. This teaching finds favor in his heart. He benefits the maximum. So says a verse in the Rigveda. It qualifies the aspirant. That is the minimum requirement.

Sitting at the Master's feet, attending his satsang regularly, listening to his discourse again and again, and keeping the mind open, the heart loving, all of this shall get you there. One-pointed commitment, the fire of passionate devotion, is the key.

Arise, Awake and Joyfully imbibe this ultimate wisdom. Prioritize to Purify thyself. The Divine is yours, Brahman is yours, Nature's forces are here to serve you.

3.2.11 Thus is recorded the Upanishad that was revealed by the great sage Angiras in the olden days.

Such is the wisdom that emanated from the one whose body was filled with nectar. Whose heart was the cradle of God. Whose limbs were fit to hold the fiery Kundalini. Whose speech was concise, convincing, and respectful.

It is pointless to discuss it without reference or proper
guidance. It becomes irrelevant for the naive, for one lacking
time or focus it carries no appeal. It is so fine and soft that it
causes no ripple in a stormy mind.

A blocked heart lacking the will should first be prepared
with a routine of proper diet, exercise, and basic education.

Step by step must one be led.
For the contented and sincere must it be shared with.
Salutations to the Great seers.
Prostrations to the Divine sages.
Deepest appreciation and grateful acknowledgement to the
indomitable Rishis.

6 The Prashna Upanishad

Shanti Mantra

oṃ bhadraṃ karṇebhiḥ śṛṇuyāma devāḥ | bhadraṃ paśye
mākṣabhir yajatrāḥ | sthirairaṅgais tuṣṭuvāṃsastanūbhiḥ |
vyaśema devahitaṃ yadāyuḥ ‖ svasti na indro vṛddhaśravāḥ
| svasti naḥ pūṣā viśvavedāḥ | svasti nastārkṣyo ariṣṭanemiḥ
| svasti no bṛhaspatirdadhātu ‖ oṃ śāntiḥ śāntiḥ śāntiḥ ‖

O Divine Wisdom!
May our ears listen to the sacred and the auspicious. May
our eyes see the propitious as we come together to partake
of wisdom.
May our limbs be firm and body attuned to long endurances.
May our senses function with full alertness and
May the sense of contentment be strong.
May our good thoughts form a discus to shield us and May
our education give us a shining personality.

Peace in our heart, in our body and in our environs.

<u>Atharva Veda = Atharvaveda Samhita + Atharvaveda Brahmana.</u>
As of today, Samhita portion is available in two recensions, namely Paippalada and Shaunaka. Brahmana portion is available in one recension only, namely Gopatha Brahmana. Prashna is attributed to sage Pippalada and is in the Gopatha Brahmana. Pippalada is the scientist who got it first, while Gopatha is the scientist who made it known to the world. The Samhita portion is the practical aspect, that details how the day's routine should be, what one should wear and when, what not to eat, which ritual to perform and how, when to sleep, etc. The Brahmana portion reflects on it and in the form of a dialogue seeks to answer the profound questions regarding existence that lead to happiness and nirvana.

Mundaka verses are actually in the earlier portion, and in the later portion are the Prashna verses. Thus Prashna contains the complete essence, including that of Mundaka. Prashna Upanishad gets its name from Prashna = "Question".

When
one's mind is peaceful,
the heart is loving,
basic needs are well taken care of,
Then
a question that arises is directly addressed by the Divine,
since it is addressed only to the Divine.

praśanopaniṣad

atha Praśna Upaniṣad

Now begins the Praśna

The Six Seekers

- Sukesha (wonderful hair, well-groomed, avoid dandruff, maintain dress code and personality) the son of Bharadvaja.
- Satyakama (truthful honest dedicated sincere in efforts) the son of Shibi.
- Sun-God's grandson (resplendent, brilliant, full of the vigor of life, fit as a fiddle) having surname Garg.
- Kausalya (healthy, pleasant and cheerful, peaceful and happy) the son of Ashvala.
- Bhargava, descendent of Bhrigu (wealthy, resourceful, centered) from Vidarbha-the center of India.
- Kabandhi, the great grandson of Katya.

In India, *Garg, Kaushal, Bhargav* are common surnames.

Qualifications Prerequisites

Respectfulness, Readiness to serve with cheerfulness, Capacity to maintain frugal discipline for one year.

1ˢᵗ Question by Kabandhi

How is the Universe sustained?
Universe is sustained by food. It is a principle that operates
in creation. There is a food-chain. Food is created,
nourishment happens and all beings get sustenance.

Name and Form = Life and Matter
Name = Life = Living Matter
Form = Matter = Cosmic Dust
Both are interconnected and tightly coupled, though we
may have only Name and only Form as well. Creation is
infinite, the Supreme loves diversity, even though a large
part adheres to some law, rare cases cannot be so confined,
this is the Beauty in Diversity.

Sunlight and Moonlight = Prana and Rayi

Southern and Northern Pathways
Pleasure and Beyond Pleasure.
The Downward and Upward Currents.

Initially our mother pampers us, with many goodies, and
running to our side when we are infants 100s of times a day.
When one is young, the neighbors and folks around us are
kind and forgiving and benevolent; society rarely enforces
laws over children.

These and such moments are collectively called the
Southern pathway, or the pleasurable journey, that is naïve,
childish forgettable. Even when one grows up, if one
continues to behave indulgingly and live in unawareness
and intoxication, then Nature steps in to punish by ruining

our health, relationships or finances. In the end, one departs regretful, sorrowful, begging pardon.

For some of us, awakening comes early. A Master, or a School, or a Colleague, or some Adventure, turns our path from pleasure to Beyond pleasure.

The moment comes when one no longer craves for pleasure. One is no longer hankering for goodies that have an iOweYou sting. One no longer relishes food that has not been honestly earned. One finds gifts and perks bothersome. One wishes to live sans entanglement. Free in Mind, Light in Heart.

This is known as the Northern pathway. The journey beyond pleasure. The life of discipline, hard work, sincerity, and self-growth.

The Vedic Rishis were seers of a high order. They used simple commonplace words to guide and teach. Many people came to them seeking advice. It was not a seeking, rather people wanted the Master to identify which of their desires was unworthy. They wished the master to stamp approval on the option that was safe and sound. The kind hearted master simply said – This is the Southern pathway, pleasurable initially and hell in the long run. That is the Northern pathway, difficult to begin with and not at all likable to the senses. Yet a path that guarantees victory in the long run.

For experiencing the truth of the Upward and Downward play of Prana, one can do Sri Sri's Chakra Meditation taught in the Advanced Meditation Course (AMC).

For experiencing and owning these fine movements and vibrations so that we can well integrate the interplay of subtle purifying currents, we may join the Sanyam Course of the Art of Living.

(Bharadvaja's son) Bhāradvaja (also known as) Sukeśā, and
(Śibi's son) Śaibya (also known as) Satyakāma, and
(grandson of Surya the Sun-god) Sauryāyaṇī (also known as) Gārgya, and
(Aśvalāya's son) Āśvalāyan (also known as) Kausalya, and
(the one from the land of Vidarbha) Vaidarbhi (also known as) Bhārgava,
(Katya's great grandson) Kātyāyana (also known as) Kabandhī,
Verily they;
those who were seeking Brahman and who were earnestly
practicing their attainment for Brahman,
in that seeking for the Ultimate Brahman,
This surely
"It all he shall expound" thus (thinking),
They-once upon a time-with due reverence, sincerity, and
willingness to serve,
approached the Sage Pippalada.

1.1 The number 6 wants to ascend to 7. Symbolically 7 is the highest state, as the sahasrara chakra. Or 7 is the maximum no of items, objectives or milestones.

A method of quality control is named Six sigma. An earthquake of 6 magnitude is considered very strong.

In cricket, a popular sport today, there are 6 balls in an over and 6 runs is the maximum hit off a ball. After 6 days of working, we earn a weekend.

Similarly 6 players make a team in volleyball. A honeycomb

is a hexagon. In IELTS, a score of 6 is the minimum requirement to apply to a top school. Mathematically 6 is a perfect number. And in Yoga, Vedanta and fitness classes, the 6th sense is a prized - to be polished - faculty.

So this Upanishad is in the form of a dialog between 6 disciples and a Master. The 6 disciples do not mean six physical bodies. Rather it points to the fact that only after one has crossed 6 milestones or 6 levels does one possess enough qualification to aspire for the ultimate.

In fact it also points to the basic principle in operation in a human socio-economic set-up. To attain to the top rung in any civil or military or spiritual context, advancing 6 levels is needed.

Another quality for the aspirant consists of the 4 personality traits:

> 1) A trustful, respectful, discriminating attitude. Viveka.
>
> 2) Showing restraint or dispassion in matters unconnected to the job. Not overstepping one's work domain. Vairagya.
>
> 3) A willingness and endurance to serve whole-heartedly for a length of time, e.g. a year or two years. Shat Sampatti.
>
> 4) A desire to learn, evolve, become more useful. Mumukshutva.

So when an aspirant has cleared 6 stages in life and his personality reflects these 4 traits, he is qualified to enter the pure Brahman space.

6 such seekers got admission to Stanford, or IIT Bombay, or

the Art of Living Ashram. They were asked to prove their mettle and display their capabilities by going through a rigorous orientation program for 12 months. The program also tested whether company policy and institute ground rules were properly adhered to by the entrants.

1.2 No promises were made, nor any hope raising by flowery language.

The gurukul had an excellent canteen that served sufficient and nutritious food at specific meal times, there were lots of physically demanding chores and running about to keep them in peak fitness, the living quarters were Spartan to prevent laziness, sloth and indulgence. The head very professionally advised them to get on with their tasks, and not to disturb him till their orientation was over.

1.3 Ka-Bandhin, the one who feels trapped, "What for this Trap?", and is always seeking to be free, was the first to complete his orientation process successfully. He ran to the Master, all quivering, and with head bowed and hands folded, stood before him.

When the great Master kindly acknowledged his presence, choosing his words carefully, Ka-Bandhi enquired. "O Great One, why do so many men and beasts and creatures take birth? Who is responsible for their sustenance? Does anyone bother to ensure their well-being?

It seems from nothing the flora and fauna is sprouting, bees and bacteria are emanating, then how is it possible that they shall find joy? What ensures that man shall experience peace? How does anyone obtain satisfaction?

1.4 The Master was not to be thwarted so easily. He got down to basic biology, and simply said - of course all creatures take birth due to the intercourse of the male and female of their species. Naturally they grow by leaps and bounds by the simple laws of mathematical division and multiplication.

To make the discussion technical and professional, the Master continued - you may consider the male sperm as a continuous moving energy beam. The female egg can be thought of as a body of matter that is impregnated and infused with life by the male energy beam falling on it.

Now as to the question of why does the energy interact with matter, the answer is ridiculously simple. For enjoyment, entertainment, and self-protection. It is for this reason we all strive to expand our holdings, stock, land and possessions.

It gives man much pleasure when his progeny increases and his wealth multiplies.

So also nature seeks to produce a variety and diversity of phenomena. By altering the strength, direction, and interplay of its energies, mother nature succeeds in spawning an amazing tapestry of all sorts of beings and matter, animate and inanimate.

And we can imagine mother nature to be united with a fatherly force, to keep the equation simple and the theory digestible.

To say that someone did something for oneself, be it profit, entertainment or pleasure, is kind of the most acceptable legal statement for a jury or judge to decide the case and put an end to further enquiry.

This is how the Master taught the boy biology, math, geography, history and law.

Obviously "the Ultimate" could not be learnt directly, but it could be catalyzed by learning everything else perfectly.

Sooner or later the seed of infinity would sprout, and the boy would attain enlightenment.

1.5 To make the discourse practical and interesting, and the concept clear; the Master gave the analogy of the Sun and the Moon. Just as the fiery sun makes us all wake up and go about our chores, and the beautiful moon provides much needed soothing rest and time for entertainment, so does mother nature synchronize both work and play.

Seemingly after birth, the father's role vanishes, the mother gets to do many tasks and provide various bells and whistles. So does Brahman recede into the background. The young children interact and grow up learning from mother, other relatives, society and environment. All of which is supposedly supervised and directed by mother's will.

1.6 Of course the brilliance is seen far and wide. Surely world champions are hailed in every nook and corner. Light travels quickly to all the four quarters, it's principles of reflection, refraction, linear motion, diffraction, diffusion, dispersion are all taught to the budding student.

And why does physics play such an elementary role? Why do all inventors, creators, and entrepreneurs emphasize the physical principles? It is something visible, interactable, and transactional. Entire economy of a company or country is based on getting the physics right. Product must be appealing, aesthetic, pleasing. So much emphasis on looks, texture, color. Almost all processed foods nowadays get a dose of coloring (artificial), even drugs and raw fruits, spices and vegetables get painted. For any home or office, the interior design is big business, it should have great color combination. Latest the automobile or gadget, funkier the colors. Dress code, fabric, machine or fashion is all about satisfying the eye.

The Master deftly explains the importance of eye, eyesight, and inner vision by drawing parallel to the glory of the sunlight and how sunRays illumine all corners of the globe.

And in the process teaches physics, thermodynamics, kinetics, also optics, communications, and importance of sunlight in life.

1.7 The Master goes on to teach the amazing use of fire in life. Forging, manufacturing, welding, cutting, molding, ignition, cooking. Almost no human activity proceeds without the direct use of fire. Even worship has a flame, a diya, agarbatti, aarti. All festivals and celebrations have candle lights and exorbitant display of lights and fireworks. Weddings don't happen without the fire ritual.

Movement of any kind, any motor vehicle is impossible without a spark.

Involuntary functions of the body, nervous system, etc. are

electric in nature, and digestion cannot proceed without a strong jathar Agni - digestive fire in the stomach.

No mobile phone, laptop, or gadget can work without electricity or battery charge. Electric energy is fast replacing combustion fuel, as evident in the highly successful Tesla Motor vehicles of Elon Musk and home solar panels. Germany is powering entire cities on solar power, the world is following suit.

1.8 Even our brain impulses are electric in nature as seen in neural activity and all thoughts arise from the sparking of 16 neurons.

Nerves are carriers of electric packet information, and the least understood of all anatomical parts.

Gold and Silver are highly prized, and are used as the currency for economic activity as well.

Every home, office, motorway, or township functions due to proper lighting and stable power supply.

Fire and its quality of light and heat that propels and causes movement, all is to be properly studied, harnessed, and made use of.

The master also emphasizes rising up at dawn and greeting the sun, and gazing lovingly at the sunset, meditating at these times.

1.9 Now the Master introduces the concept of Time. Seconds, minutes, hours. Day, week, month, season, year.

All based on the movement of the sun. The humble clock, wristwatch or alarm chime, these govern each and every action of man. No smart phone or computer has been invented that does not use a clock processor chip. And none shall be sold if it does not display the time and date. Our waking, eating, working, sleeping all are time dependent. Our education system has the daily period, monthly timetable, and yearly task scheduler.

What exactly is Time? We can think in the fraction of a second, and remember or imagine events and places far separated in Time. Time hangs heavy during sorrow, and flies gaily during joy. Time makes and breaks relationships, officers get thrown out or penalized for not maintaining the time.

For babies and young children time is not of any great relevance. Animals and plants are not so aware or bothered with time. Inanimate objects and things, furniture and walls and flooring, couldn't care less about time.

How Real is Time, and how much should it intrude our lives? The master discussed all such matters, including duty, responsibility, honesty, discipline and regularity in practice. A stich in time saves nine. Nip the evil in the bud. Early to bed early to rise makes a man healthy, wealthy and wise.

1.10 Followers of time discipline have much to look forward to and rejoice. Their happy moments, eureka phases and "we did it" exultations far outnumber those peoples who behave callous w.r.t. time.

Frequently we have heard the phrase in sport - he sweet times the ball, his timing is perfect. And in all running or swimming or cycling or racing contests, the man who has the best time wins.

Importance of time has been highlighted. Tributes are paid to those who live according to the season and occasion. This is what makes a well-groomed personality that is respected by all.

Timing is inbuilt in our para-sympathetic systems. Heartbeat, hormone release, digestion all run on time for a fit person. Such a person performs well in the world and is regarded as a pillar of society, a model citizen worth emulating.

Even celestial bodies, the sun and moon, have a rhythm in their movement. We all know at what time the sun will rise and set.

Dance, Orchestra, Symphony, Choir, time lends grace to all, great timing is what makes them extraordinary.

The disciple is given no chance of not incorporating timeliness in life. Planning, programming, goal setting, prioritizing, making any event a success requires meticulous adherence to time.

And what of those who have a respect for time and timeliness? This Upanishad verse says -

- They are the real champions.
- They are the most honored.
- Their health and fitness is superior since their breath is unhurried.
- They have no fear, nor any guilt. Untimeliness and procrastination become the biggest source of deep-rooted self-blame, which they never fall prey to.

- Their presence is valued, much sought for.
- Whoever seeks to emulate them also crosses over the shores of suffering.

This is the central teaching. This is a fundamental rule to incorporate in life.

1.11 Summer Winter Monsoon Autumn and Spring - fivefold is the time planned to aid each soul's temperament. Within the five seasons are the twelve months proportioned, so that man may seek to spend his days wisely and maximize his time in creative endeavors.

Each founding father of a successful organization rotates his employees, chooses his company locations, and shares his wisdom equally amongst his upper echelon executives.

Further, the time has been divided into 7 days in a week for all types of works, jobs, offices and schools, with 6 days of mandatory attendance. This system of time has gotten unqualified approval throughout the ages.

All quarters including the military have sought to give a breather or time for introspection and rejuvenation, to staff and students as the weekly holiday.

1.12 Months have been divided into fortnights, specially taking into consideration the waxing and the waning moon. The waning moon fortnight is more suited to the feminine qualities, while the waxing moon fortnight favors masculine traits.

This simply means that each soul has a mix of the tender feminine virtues - grace, emotional bonding, teamwork, flexibility, sensitivity; and the assertive masculine virtues - clarity, focus, mission completion, endurance, bravery. These phases of the moon, viz. The dark fortnight is especially suited to enhancing feminine virtues, while the bright fortnight is more helpful in nurturing masculine traits. The energy content of the moonlight has been studied and analyzed in depth by the Master, who then trains disciples according to which traits of theirs need polishing.

Medical science has progressed to the extent whereby the effects of the new moon and the full moon on the mind have been understood. Also the scientists have observed the beneficial effects of fasting on ekadashi or the 11th day of the moon's cycle. Many agriculturists and farmers are beginning to incorporate the age-old wisdom of sowing, harvesting, and rotating crop cycles as per the phases of the moon.

The nutritional quality of herbs, fruits, and vegetables has been found to be greatly affected by moonlight. Some exotic and rare flowers bloom only at night during the moonlight. Some potent formulations, e.g. making kheer on the full moon night of Sharad Poornima, has become a patent ritual considering its confirmed benefits.

Day and Night it has been said; the Lord's Day is similar to movement i.e. earning. Likewise his Night is akin to rest and enjoyment.
Stamina surely they dissipate theirs who during daytime desiring love unite in embrace,
while
Wholesome certainly theirs love who during nighttime for desiring each other have intercourse.

Can we make love anytime?

The master who has a thorough understanding of anatomy, our body's internal design, and the physiological processes predominant during daylight and nighttime, has a simple answer.
Cohabitation makes sense during nighttime since
- that will protect the body,
- maintain one's immunity, and
- be certainly more enjoyable in the ambient conditions prevailing during the night.

1.13 And may we salute the day, and pay our respects to the night too, for each has been designed by the Lord for distinctly different activities, to match the design of our anatomy and our brain. Eyesight is supremely connected to sunlight, so also the Vitamin D needed by the body. A regular dose of sunlight will accordingly maintain our vision and strength. Watching the stars and the moonlight, gazing at the dawn and the sunset, empowers us in many ways. These cosmic energies intimately impinge on the body and the mind.

A further point to note is the importance of acts to be done in daytime and in nighttime. The act of copulation is expressly to be done in seclusion, considering it to be most intimate and affecting the brain and physiology greatly. Nighttime or the soft moonlight is much more conducive for physical intimacy as it closely matches the energy spectrum of the brain and biorhythm of the body. This helps in maintaining body fluid balance. Conjugal union at night alone keeps one fit physically, keeps one's emotions healthy, and prevents one's senses from straying unduly.

This information is based on time-tested medical principles of human anatomy, physiology, and psychology. Thus the Upanishad gives clear guidelines to couples for health and happiness in married life, and also for begetting robust children.

1.14 Food certainly (is) the Lord of all,

Food - good, fresh, nutritious food that gels with your system. Eat such foodstuffs regularly. Eat with respect, honor, and gratefulness. Get proper advice regarding diet. Have the judicious mix of carbohydrates, proteins, vitamins, minerals, fiber from natural foods itself. The Rishi says naturally grown items are compatible with the human system. Eating pills and vitamins is not of much use, since there is only a slim chance that your system can process it.

The presence of sunlight and moonlight, and the appropriate temperature, humidity, pressure, all of these along with the natural soil is what makes the proteins and vitamins digestible - Agreeable to the muscles, bones and nerves - Satiating to the soul. The stuff nature grows no factory can grow. Wait till you get an Android body before you start eating factory made chemicals.

And the story doesn't end here. Sooner or later you might marry. And likely have a baby. Do you have any clue at all as to how a baby is made? Can factories make babies. Not just yet. Prevent continuous contract with the medics and lifelong illnesses.

The Rishi clearly says in this verse, for babies to be born

error free, illness free, cheerful, healthy and strong, please eat nature's bounty farm fresh.

1.15 For sure. It is certain. Those who follow:
- Farm fresh foods in proper quantity and nutritious mix as per recommended diet
- Conjugal union at nighttime only, as it inhibits loss of essential fluids and bone marrow. It Avoids weakening of muscles and nerves, and helps maintain hormonal balance.
- Proper exposure to sunlight. Proper exposure to moonlight. Enough fresh air.

It is guaranteed their married life shall withstand all storms. It is certified their family shall have harmony, hearty emotional bonding, enough excitement and joys. Their progeny shall inherit a value system of Truthfulness, Discipline, Commitment. They shall attain heavenly Bliss in this life.

1.16 The Master goes on to enumerate the fruits for those aspirants who prefer to remain unmarried. For those of us who prefer not to raise a family. For those who keep aloof from flirting, follow the principles of honest hard-work, and take out enough time for wholesome exercise. Well, such folk too taste the heavenly Bliss. They also taste the joys, excitement, happiness. They also keep robust health. Respect and Stature in society is theirs. Goodwill and Trust enrich their lives.

Thus the Master taught his talented student Reading-Writing-Arithmetic. Personality and Character development. Ethics and Mental toughness in one's workplace. Robust health guidelines. Raising a family and finding Bliss in life.

2nd *Question by Bhargav*

a. Which energies operate inside a Being?
The 5 elements, the 5 senses, Mind and the Breath.
b. How are these energies sustained?
These are all sustained by the Life force we breathe in.
c. Which of these is the principal energy?
The Breath is the principal energy.

Prana = Life Force = Power of Breath

2.1 Full of respect and with a sense of awe, the next disciple named Bhargava approached the Master.

He was from Vidarbha or the central Indian Deccan plateau, a region known for harsh weather; and wished to know the science behind luck and good fortune.

He enquired humbly - O Merciful Lord! Please guide us regarding the seemingly unequal distribution of wealth, resources, joys and successes in this world. Who controls what? How does a body get what it needs for existence?

And his final query - which principle is the primary key to man's survival and fitness?

2.2 The Master welcomed this strange yet serious question. Willingly he replied - The control of each resource lies with the governing heads of the five elements of which this physical creation is composed of. The five elements are the Space, Air, Fire, Water and Earth. Each element reports to its chief executive officer who is appointed by the Divine Mother.

Additionally the physical creation is infused with intelligence that is commonly known by the sense organs and the reasoning faculty. These all similarly report to their individual presiding officer appointed by the Divine Mother.

The five elements and the processing brain are actually dumb, they simply function as per a set plan with no desire nor notion beyond the obvious. Eating Sleeping Mating Possessing seem to rule everybody. Everyone is trying to look outside and run his affairs based on external appearances. It is hard to find someone who is purifying his innards - developing Kindness Acceptance Belongingness Humility.

And so man keeps spending on the body, senses, and feeding information to the brain. These rule him and by various opportune means signal their importance to him.

2.3 The mightiest of them all - the Breath – counseled,

"Do not spend all your time and money and effort in illusory pursuit".

"In breath is the secret of life, its regulation holds the key to materialistic success and also to spiritual attainment".

"Bodily functions proceed well with deep rhythmic breathing. All mental faculties are kept alert by Pranayama. The 5 major involuntary systems - Respiration, Circulation, Digestion, Excretion and Immunity - are ably supported by various components of the breath".

"You must follow a discipline of Yoga, Pranayama, Walking, and Outdoor activity in fresh air".

Naturally for the busy goal-oriented fellows, this plea fell on deaf ears. It didn't deter the breath, it knew the brave, the noble, the successful, and those gifted with divine vision would always have top priority for Pranayama and Meditation.

2.4

It due to being offended (by their vanity) got up and set out to depart as if,

in its departing all the others also lose consciousness, while

in its firmly staying all function well.
The situation is akin to the bees; when the queen bee takes off all also take off, in its staying put all also stay put;

Hence the tongue-mind-eye-and-ear, they having been given ample proof;

the life breath they all glorify.

For the pompous, the cruel, or the obstinate, breath becomes shallow, laborious, and feverish. With its fluctuating and miss-timing, the other parameters of the body also become weakened.

Body and senses function well so long as the breath is taken care of. When pranayama is neglected, when outdoor sports and activities are shunned, the body loses immunity and quickly becomes prey to all sorts of illnesses.

Health departs as breath becomes unregulated, life itself

bids adieu when the breath leaves.

At such times by a stroke of grace, man renews his friendship with the breath. He steadies himself, re-plans and reprioritizes. He seeks to learn breathing techniques.

Then his speech and intellect start making statements in praise of breath. Then his sight begins to enjoy Yoga, his hearing finds the temple Chants and Bhajans, sounds of Bhastrika and Kriya sweetest.

2.5

This fire energizes
the sun, the cloud, the senses controller, and the air.
This animates the earth, the matter, the subtle energies,
It infuses the real and the imaginary, and the eternal,
whatever that is.

Suddenly man realizes the truth. What he failed to notice as he kept racing along the raging torrents of social affairs, when he finally got thrown in, it was grace that opened his eyes.

He goes slow and steady, he becomes cultured and reverential, he begins to live when his breathing pattern gets restored to his childhood days.

He notices everything with wonder. The plants and flowers. The bushes and trees. The lakes and rivers. The food and the family members, all seem Divine. The earth and the air become sacred. The fires become godly as he participates in Havan and Yagya.

He begins to acknowledge the presence of the almighty. His

bitterness and frustration give way to awe and glee.

He senses the divine in peoples and objects. He senses the invisible superior consciousness.

He starts to make his first baby- like innocent movements on the road devoid of lack, on the path that knows no grief.

2.6

Just as the spokes of the chariot wheel keep it together,

Likewise in the life-force everything is fitted —
Be it the cosmos, the society, the individual, every endeavor,
the ruler and the discerning saint or scholar.

The supreme secret of pranayama dawns. The real truth of life unfolds and it begins to flow meaningfully, just as the car tire glides smoothly when correctly pressurized and kept clean.

Yoga studios and Naturopathy become the fashion.
Inner beauty blossoms when in
- Family, Work, or Play,

In each of these, Pranayama practice is made a default activity.

2.7

O Breath! You are just like the great creator. The beating heart confirms thy presence. The moving life-force in the womb signals by means of encouraging kicks - O it's such a delight when a newborn greets the air and motherhood is born. You take lungfulls of breath. You make the parents feel as if their likeness has arrived. O what a

Blessing to hear you move. To hear the steady pulse.

Everyone respects life. All of nature rejoices when life is born, whether gazelle, calf, cub or flower. Various and multifarious are the celebrations and parties. Living beings are recognized by the moving life energy in them.

2.8
Of the subtle energies you are the fastest,
Of the bodiless beings the first contact.
Of the Sages the pure character and true strength,
Of worldly beings the simple joy and contentment
Thee are.

As we are getting the drift, Prashna Upanishad is stamping the superiority of Breath. Why? So that man learns a Pranayama technique, cultivates it with patience, and then sticks to it by incorporating the Kriya in daily life. Not like bathing or brushing rush jobs, not like fast-food on the go stuffing, not like popping a tablet to get rid of a headache or overcome insomnia. No Sir.

Not in any jerky, time tacky, passionless manner. Nope. That does not qualify as Pranayama. That is not Sudarshan Kriya.

To make the seeker aware of the inner truth is the prime focus of Prashna. It goes on in this verse to extol beautiful aspects of the Life Force.

Prana is the fastest, the first to reach the brain. Of all forces and fluids in the body, the prana reaches all cells before anything else. It nourishes, supports, and facilitates each organ best. Hence foremost amongst all Shaktis. Of all energies the greatest.

Of every guest of honor, prana is introduced the first, so that it starts to flow in everyone smoothly, and all proceedings progress without a hitch.

Prana is the "Atharvan" = the simplest, lightest and easiest to regulate. The one requiring least effort and expense to maintain and keep healthy, of all limbs and of all sense organs.

The reality and personality of creation thee are O Prana!

The prime factor in all of creation. The one mark of "he moves thus he is alive and well".

So much emphasis on the Prana in this Upanishad.

- So that it gets firmly etched in the brain.
- It becomes a lifelong habit.
- It evokes awe, respect, belongingness, ownership.
- It becomes invaluable. It becomes priceless.

It achieves the status of:
"COME WHAT MAY,
I SHALL DO MY PRANAYAMA.
I SHALL DO MY SUDARSHAN KRIYA.
I SHALL DO IT SINCERELY. WITH ALL RESPECT. WITH ALL STEPS IN PROPER SEQUENCE. IN COMPLETENESS AS MY MASTER TAUGHT".

When you shower on all these O Breath! they the creatures, in delight remain hopeful, that to their heart's desire grain and nourishment shall be had.

2.9

By your superfine sublimity you govern the sense organs –
"Indra".

By your flowing and nourishing nature like "Rudra", you
strengthen and protect the body-Mind.

You are the steady wind required for incessant combustion
and fusion in the heavenly Sun.

You Lord over all flames by being their O_2 line.

2.10 And the magic happens. Clouds form, air currents
transport heavy rain bearing clouds to distant farmlands
earnestly seeking, their bellies starving.

Clouds burst, Rains come, and in no time the life-giving
nectar gives rise to unbridled joy.

Insects. humans, otters, seals, bears salmon, cows ducks,
geese, tigers, babies, newborns, all experience the thrill of
fresh life.

Nature rejoices, there is Bliss all around. Grain is there to
gladden the heart, Milk is sweet to nourish the soul. Food a
plenty is there for all.

2.11 O Life force! Thee are uninitiated, the first-light giver,
just as dawn or the lamp that is lit at dusk. Dawn doesn't
have light before, the first lamp that is kindled doesn't have
any lamp put on before it, so uninitiated the firstborn, due
to whose birth and movement inside the body one senses
life for the first time. A baby becomes alive due to the prana,

and it experiences all due to the breath.

O Breath! Thee are that which initiates Digestion, that which starts Metabolism, that which causes Ignition.

O Air! You are Earth's tight hug,
- as a man's bride.
- as a woman's hubby.
- as one's closest companion.

Waking up we all gulp you in, we become aware we are alive, we honor thee with Chants, Pranayama, Meditation, Ozone air garden walks.

O Prana! More than a loving mother, indeed you are our father as well.

2.12 O dear breath! Thou who art firmly flowing in this body and making us hear and see and reason; Make it all auspicious, make us pure, make us divine.

Please do not forsake this body, please do not even consider departure.

Life is so precious, do not quit. The cosmos is made alive by thine presence, keep moving.

2.13 Verily O Breath! You move in the triumvirate - body, mind, heart. All are dependent upon thee, every human is under your thumb. We all function because of your availability.

Just as a mother protects her young children so do thee

ensure our well-being.

O Divine Force! Provide us with sound health, handsome complexion, a sharp brain.

Kindly see to it that we learn to regulate the breath
- so as to live well,
- function ably, and
- rise to stature and respectability in society.

3rd *Question by Kauśal*

a. What causes the Life force?
The Brahman Shiva consciousness.
b. How does it function within the Being?
As five Prana Vayus and five Upaprana Vayus.
c. How does it depart?
By means of the Udana Vayu, the Last thought rules.
d. What is the cosmic energy?
An intelligent energy that is enlivened by Prana the life force.
e. Can it unveil the Soul?
Its awareness through grace helps reveal the Soul.

3.1 And Now after the earlier quest has been satisfactorily addressed, and the previous thought wave has been quenched.

There is a new surge of fresh current.
The stormy fleet-footed horse-like,
The highly observant all talented wave like energy bursts upon the scene.

In a flurry quest gets tabled, building upon the foundation so far made. 1. How does Life Force = the Prana come into existence? 2. How doth the Breath get tightly coupled to the limp Body? 3. How does it separate into the various functions of respiration, circulation, evacuation, and the rest? How does it enter into the flirting of the senses? How causes it dilly-dallying of reason? How brings it upheaval in memory? Why causes it Ego to harden?

By what mechanism does Prana exit the body?
How does it function externally as cosmic energy to sustain the galaxies and planetary systems?

Really how does it get the power to unveil the soul?

Prana Vayu and Upaprana Vayu

3.2 The Master spoke in a tone of caressing benevolence –

You ask deep fundamental questions. Questions that never occur to the ordinary student.

Much mature yet equally humble art thee. Keen yet sure-footed, bold and incisive, impatient but not awkward your tone.

Hence, I shall certainly address your queries, well may they all be resolved.

3.3 This life energy is an offshoot of Brahman, the Shiva consciousness. Prana is the silent shady envelope. It is the caressing, constantly comforting, undeniable aspect of God. It is as if the power of God extended in creation. it is the link between mind and body. It is what ties a pure soul to the complex mind and yokes it to the body. It is as though a projection of the soul that desires to enjoy and experience. It is the reflection of life.

Prana links the mighty Sun's soul-rays to innumerable multifaceted dust particles, infusing each with godliness, making each alive.

"Chaaya" = Resemblance, Reflection, Shadow. Life is the Reflection of the Soul. Prana is the undeniable proof of Life. Just as we know someone is Alive due to the movement of the Breath, similarly **by the working of his Mind** we know that he is unique, distinct, and separate from the rest.

We have two interpretations of this powerful word. One interpretation is that the Brahman desires infinitely, and that leads to life, a composite of soul+mind+body all linked together by the breath. Brahman then plays its leela in various bodies, and after sometime it all resolves back. Then the cycle continues indefinitely…

The Karmic Impression Driving Force

Another interpretation is that Brahman simply divides infinitely, and then each soul has a free-will that is _as if governed_ by the component called mind. Due to the mind's willing, the soul gets attached to specific bodies by the breath, enjoys for a while, then goes for a new body. After some cycles of enjoying in various bodies, it somehow gets the grace to align with the supreme. This is the theory of Karma.

Delegate and Relax

3.4 Just as a Father delegates responsibility to his progeny,

- just as a President divides the work according to the skills of his secretaries,
- just as flowers bloom according to the seasons and tributaries branch out from the mighty Ganges,
- just as one fertilized egg gets differentiated into eyes, hands, heart or bone,

So does the life force split into various currents. Each current is wholly independent, responsible, and cut out for its work.

Prana Apana Samana Vyana Udana
Naga Kurma Devadatta Krikala Dhananjaya

The five Prana Vayu - Prana, Apana, Udana, Vyana and Samana.

The five Upaprana Vayu - Naga, Kurma, Devadatta, Krikala and Dhananjaya.

3.5

THROAT Vishuddhi Chakra- Udana Vayu Immunity
HEART   Anahata Chakra-   Prana Vayu Respiration
NAVEL   Manipura Chakra-   Samana Vayu Digestion
WHOLE   Swadisthana Chakra-Vyana Vayu Circulation
PELVIS Mooladhara Chakra- Apana Vayu Evacuation

In the organs of excretion, and in the organs of pleasurable sex and reproduction; the energy current is named Apana.

This Apana is a specific and distinct portion of the Life Force (Prana) that flows vertically downwards in the body. Together with the mouth and nose in the region of the face consisting of the senses, the eyes, ears, etc., the energy

current is named the same as itself viz. Prana. This Prana is a specific and distinct portion of the Life Force (Prana) that flows vertically upwards in the body.

The life force is thus split into 5 vayus for efficient governance. And it also gives rise to the 7 energy centers or chakras that regulate the being. Seven luminous flames. Chakras are "luminous" meaning functional, "flames" meaning powerful.

72000 Nadis each in 100 of 101

3.6 The Soul is situated in the physical heart.
Here branching out of nerves. From the heart region, 101 major tubular channels reach out to all parts of the Being. Each of these 101 trunk lines contains 100 branches. Each of the 100 branches contains 72000 nadi, i.e. 101x100x72000=72,72,00,000=72crore & 72lakh nadi.

Sum Total of all large and medium and fine nadi = 101+10100+727200000 = 72,72,10,201.
72 crore 72 lakh 10 thousand 2 hundred and 1.

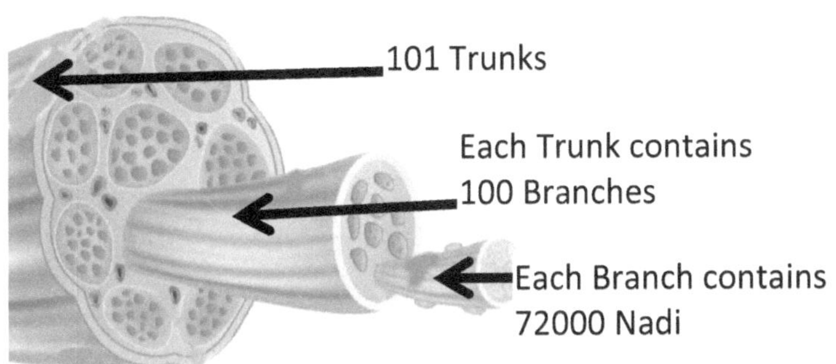

Within these nadis, the "Vyana" Vayu moves. These are the arteries and veins of the circulatory system on the physical level. And the nerve pathways for the mind on the subtle level. And for the soul on the causal level.

Note – Some of these pathways may have only one function, others may have multiple. The identification and tagging of each nadi is done elsewhere in the Veda.

Pipal tree analogy. Heart is the Pipal Tree.
After a few years, many trunks grow out, consider that 101 trunks grow out.

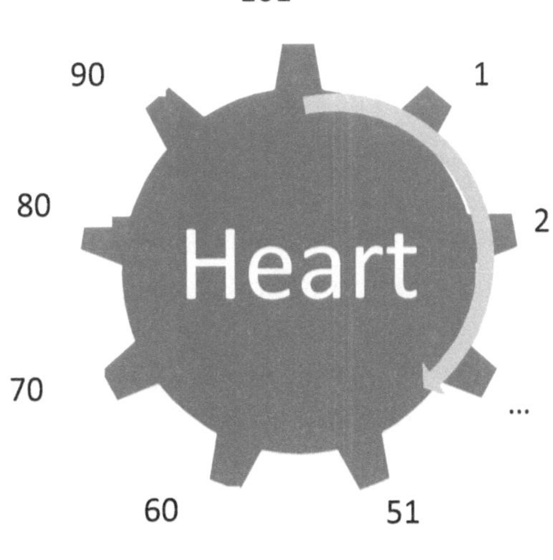

213 Prashna

So now we have 101 trunks, and each trunk has 100 branches, as a thumb rule.

Of course, each branch will have many twigs and there are 72000 twigs in each branch.

Significance of 72000
72 = 1x72, 2x36, 3x24, 4x18, 6x12, 8x9.
- 36 is the number that represents all the Shaktis in creation, where the highest number 36 represents Shiva consciousness.
- 24 represents the Gayatri meter.
- 18 is the number that represents all the virtues of Devi.
- 12 is the number that represents all the constellations of the Zodiac, or possibilities for mind to be stabilized or distracted.
- 9 is the highest digit in the decimal system.
- 8 is the number that represents Infinity.

Since creation is a duality principle, 36x2 = 72. And the other numbers to allow for all possibilities for karmic theory to operate, and all probable paths to liberation.

3.7 Now, the "Udana" Vayu up and beyond carries, (the soul with mind and memory and impressions and learning and leanings) the subtle and causal bodies.
One who is by virtue pure and divine, for him the exit is by the Sushumna nadi, i.e. to merge in Brahman, from where there is no return, no further cycle of birth and death = no further cycle of hate, guilt, delusion, distraction.

One who is by deeds the great, him to the world of celestial happiness = reborn as a star or celebrity = reborn as a rich and famous personality.

The unjust to the world of misery = reborn or fallen into abject poverty, illness and misfortune.

The middling to the world of humans = reborn as an average individual with plans and struggle, delights and distraction.

Light Earth Space Air

3.8 A verse that explains the functioning of the cosmos w.r.t. the five prana vayu studied earlier.

Prana Vayu in its external nature is equated to the Sun and sunlight, as it energizes the eyes and bestows sight to all.

Apana Vayu in its external nature is equated to the Earth goddess, the strong loving gravitational pull that keeps us firmly anchored.

Samana Vayu in its external nature is equated to the vast Space, with billions of stars, galaxies, clusters, and cosmic dust.

Vyana Vayu in its external nature is equated to Air and atmosphere, that which keeps the heart pumping, keeps all bodies alive.

As microcosm so the macrocosm *yat piṇḍe tat brahmāṇḍe.*

Water

3.9 What carries the soul? Don't we say Water is Amrita, the Nectar. Doesn't a parched land give infinite blessings when the rain falls? Doesn't milk gratify the soul of each being?

Udana Vayu in its external nature is equated to H_2O, that which restores man, tree, flower or machine.

Note —Tejas in other contexts is also translated as Life, luster, or Fire. In this context its meaning "Life" is apt. This completes the discussion on the five elements that compose as well as govern creation. Since 4 elements have already been said, the 5th is water.

Further, when the waters have run dry, life diminishes and ebbs away. As evident in deserts that teem with oases during the monsoons, and become empty lands during other times.

Mind bundled together with the senses, baggage packed with the emotions, impressions, and learning,

life departs from this body, and after a while, elsewhere, it springs anew.

This is commonplace as evident in the migratory birds, salmon fishes, corals, and hunters.

Final Thought Rules
This which in_the_thought is (at the hour of death, that strong desire is bundled and) led by the Prana.

Prana (= Life force) with_the_Tejas (= Udana Vayu) being
united, and with the Soul (inner being),
as strongly wished (in the end moment),
to (an another) world carries.

3.10 This verse is a Maha Vakya. It is a Supreme statement.
It states an inviolable truth.

At the hour of Death, the Thought predominant in the mind
becomes the Basis for the new birth, i.e. governs the
parameters like place of birth, parents, resources, happiness
and further evolution.

This is easily verified by observing and noting down the last
thought at bedtime. First thought in the morning while getting
up shall be the same.

Another example is that we might be thinking, "Shall I go to
Bombay or shall I go to Ambernath? Shall I wear this dress or
that"? In the end where I go and what I wear is determined by
the final thought. This is so evident is everyday life in all matters
and in all decisions.

Benefits of Upanishad

3.11 the mature one who thus understands the working of
the Prana,
his progeny, family, village and neighborhood never comes
to ruin, knows no grief, he becomes immortal, he is revered
and his life becomes the ideal for countless generations.

that is the essence of this verse which is also elucidated in
the next verse.

This summarizes the benefits of understanding life in a bigger context and leading a visionary life accordingly. This is the Upanishad in practice.

Learn Sudarshan Kriya = Master the Breath

3.12 In-depth knowledge of the Breath.

Its origin, the inhalation and exhalation speed, depth, and timing, the placement and importance of the 7 chakras,

and its relation and functioning in the 5 major systems (respiration, excretion, digestion, circulation, immunity vis-a-vis endocrine),

and thus, having known one's soul, what it is and what it takes to reveal it,

a human attains immortality. Reaches over to the plane of happiness. Crosses the dangerous self-defeating waters. Rises above hatred, suspicion, guilt, and bitterness. Becomes freed from self-imposed prison.

"again repeated" to give force to this statement. To give surety.

Full Stop. End of this teaching. End of this term. End of this class. Break for now.

4th *Question by Garg*
What is Sleep? What is Dream?
Very well explained here.

Sleeping Awake Dreaming Comfort

Four distinct words. All mean "it". However in Vedic usage, there is an added sense of the relative separation from "it". The distance is not really physical. The separation is an emotional distance or the distance for one's thought to travel. As an analogy, consider the separation of one's dress, one's skin, one's heart and one's ego from the Soul. To quantify these distances, Vedic terminology uses

- "Tat" for dress (far away from oneself)

- "Atat" for skin (close by)

- "Idam" for heart (really close)

- "Adas" for ego (oneself)

4.1 Now, the Grandson of Surya the sun-god, of the dynasty of Garg = Gārgya, specially asked this:

O Lord! Inside this being who sleeps?

Within who is awake?

Which of the two beings sees dreams? (Whether the one that sleeps or the one that is awake).

Of whose the pleasure and comfort experience is?

In what are all humans well established?

Deep Sleep State

4.2 He to him replied. (The Master answered the disciple).

O Garg! Just as in the setting of the Sun,

all the sunrays of this fiery orb become withdrawn,
and again with the rising of the sun
they once more shine forth,

Similarly all folk in the supreme being become resolved.

 It is the mind that shuts down, it is the mental faculties that come to a standstill in the Brahman. (Just as our thoughts slowdown in the presence of the Master, just as we are left speechless, thoughtless in Guruji's presence).

Indeed the state in which a person

hears not, sees not, smells not, tastes not, touches not, speaks not even a little, eats not, displays excitement not, evacuates not, roams not

then he sleeps;
thus the wise say.

Tretagni = Garhapatya-Dakshinagni-Ahavaniya

4.3 During deep sleep state;

Inside this city (body-mind complex of the person)
the currents of Prana alone are awake, up and about.
- the Apana Vayu is verily the housemaid, cleaning away all the leftover thoughts and emotions;
- the Vyana Vayu is verily the incessant circulation, doing its task meticulously;
- which from the cleaned mind (due to Apana Vayu) breathes,
- that Prana Vayu now respires cheerfully, restoring the mind's confidence and vision.

During a Yagya, a large Homa spread over several days, e.g. the Navaratri or Somayagya, three homa kunds are especially made to honor the Vayus. These are accordingly named "Garhapatya Agni" to honor Apana Vayu, "Dakshin Agni" to honor Vyana Vayu, and "(Ahavaniya Agni" to honor Prana Vayu.

Honoring is the key in festivals and celebrations. Honoring leads to all round bliss, growth and success.

4.4 Just as exhalation and inhalation are both needed to maintain proper balance, so is the functioning of Samana Vayu that digests equitably as needed; in this respect the Samana Vayu is like the officiating chief priest in a Yagya who directs each offering properly.

Note – Since Homa, Fire Ritual, Yagya are the events that bind a family together, maintain unity and harmony in a village, so the Upanishad uses it as an analogy to highlight and explain in detail the functioning of the breath. This level of detail for the breath is given so that Man can implement Pranayama in daily life. The power of breath is repeatedly told; it is to bring man's focus and attention to learn Yogic breathing techniques (like the Sudarshan Kriya in the 21st century).

The mind is verily balanced by the Udana Vayu that provides immunity, just as the Organizer of a Yagya gets the credit for ensuring safety in society.
He delivers the chosen fruit to (the organizer) this organized body-mind complex, day by day eventually leads man towards liberation.

Man might take a few life-times to attain Nirvana. Each exit of man from one body to another is enforced by the Udana Vayu.

The Udana Vayu safely transports the soul along with the mind in its current state of evolution, each time, in each birth.

Dream State

4.5 The human being while in the dream state, glory and grandeur experiences.

whichever sights and scenes man hath previously seen he conjures to see,

whatever sounds and noises man hath previously heard he conjures to hear,

and in various lands whatever his senses sought and his reasoning established, again and again in varying fashion he replays those moments up close in dreams.

The seen and never seen before,
The heard and never heard before,
The experienced and never experienced,
The real and unreal,
all such events he sees fancifully in the dreams.

The doer, the lead actor he himself becoming, all dreams he enjoys.

Comfort State

4.6 In the flash of a moment, the dream shuts off, and the human being in this body feels comforted. Experiences pleasurable bliss. A state of restful joy pervades his being.

4.7 O dear child! Just as birds retire to their chosen tree for the night,

similarly, a time comes when all beings fall in the state of deep sleep, they disconnect from the mind and senses and memories, and they experience deep rest.

Note – The Upanishad is simply expressing a forgotten fact. Each one of us, whether mighty or forlorn, whether bird or bee, plant or animal, each and every being at one point or another experiences the state of comforting rest.

For the saint this is a common thing, for animals and plants also it is quite commonplace. Only for mankind it seems to be forgotten, rare, and elusive. Still it happens.

The state of non-anxiety, the state of calmness, this pristine state of non-doership has been bestowed on all beings in creation.

Physical Elements & Subtle Counterparts

4.8 the solid earth and the subtle earth element that is present in everything including the mind,

the flowing waters and the subtle water element that is present in everything including the mind,

the physical fire and the subtle fire element that is present in everything including the mind,

the effervescent air and the subtle air element that is present in everything including the mind,

the vast space and the subtle space element that is present in everything including the mind,

the beautiful eyes and the visible objects and the act of
seeing that is a faculty of the mind,

the physical ears and the heard sounds and the act of
hearing that is a faculty of the mind,

the pesky nose and the inhaled fragrances and the act of
smelling that is a faculty of the mind,

the smooth tongue and the tasty delicacies and the act of
tasting that is a faculty of the mind,

the tender skin and the contacted beings and the act of
touching that is a faculty of the mind,

the sharp tongue and the elaborate speeches and the act of
speaking that is willed by the mind,

the firm hands and the grasped gadgets and the act of
grasping that is willed by the mind,

the conjugal organ and the pleasure giving partner and the
act of making love that is willed by the mind,

the evacuating organs and the evacuee and the act of
evacuation that is willed by the mind,

the sturdy feet and the swift movements and the act of
travelling that is willed by the mind,

the sensing mind and the sensed thoughts and the act of
thinking that is willed by the self,

the sane intellect and the pragmatic decision making and
the act of reasoning that is willed by the self,

the impartial ego and the discriminations and the act of
mineness that is willed by the self,

the full memory and the storehouse of emotions and the act
of remembering that is willed by the self,

the essential wisdom and the known and the act of knowing
that is willed by the self,

the life and the living and the act of sustenance that is willed
by the self,
...

Individual Soul - Collective Consciousness

4.9 Verily he the Seer, the Experiencer, the Listener, the
Smeller, the Taster, the thought bundle, the Judge, the
Doer, the intelligent Soul, the Being,

He; in the beyond, in the eternal, in the Supreme
Consciousness, is well absorbed - perfectly merged.

4.10 Verily that person who -
this undifferentiated, unembodied, unbiased, brilliant,
imperishable soul recognizes,

That person with the unfathomable eternal soul attains
oneness.

O dear one! definitely the one who likewise understands this
teaching he becomes omniscient, he becomes omnipresent.

THAT, this verse summarizes, and it is also elucidated in the next verse.

4.11 Wherein all beings endowed with the Prana Vayus and the five elements are well contained,

O gentle boy! certainly the wise man who THAT imperishable soul glimpses,

He, the omniscient one, is hailed as the one who has permeated the entire creation.

full stop. End of the class. End of this teaching.

5th Question by Satyakama

How is the primal sound OM relevant?
Very well explained here.

5.1 In due sequence then Satyakama the righteous, the son of Shibi, devotedly enquired regarding this topic:

O All Knowing One! Amongst all humans he who regularly till his last breath,
THAT OM the Primal Sound earnestly and properly chants and meditates upon,

he to which meritorious plane attains?

This is all I wish to know, nothing else.

To him (Satyakama) he (the master Pippalada) replied gladdened.

5.2 O Righteous One! O what of OM! The luxurious, the abundant, the all fulfilling divine…
THIS certainly is the transcendental Brahman and the worldly great as well.
Hence a sincere practitioner,
by its help one of the two wonderful planes wins.

OM - its first matra "Amm"

5.3 If he the first matra earnestly practices and meditates upon,

he by it surely realizes a most wonderful thing. Quickly it is guaranteed in this world he attains a high and wealthy position due to his earnest endeavor.

The sacred hymns describing the inviolable cosmic laws propel him to the elite class.

There he by hard-work, by balanced lifestyle, by faith and trust, luxurious living attains.

Very quickly, the person achieves a big status. It is guaranteed that greatness will come to him.

By meditating on the first matra "Amm" with attention on the Manipura Chakra, the cosmic laws get revealed as described in the Rigveda. The theoretical mind becomes sharp. Mathematical concepts become well understood. Thereby a person's talents shine and he attains to wealth and fame in the world of men.

He adheres to the laws and customs of good citizenship, this is
the reason his talents propel him to the elite class in society.

OM - its second matra "Umm"

5.4 However some men wish for bigger roles than that.

By sincerely practicing and meditating on
- the first matra "Am" with attention on the Manipura
Chakra at the Navel, and also
- the second matra "Umm" with attention on the
Anahata Chakra at the Heart

the cosmic laws get revealed as described in the Yajurveda.
The practical mind becomes sharp. Physics and Chemistry
become well understood.

Thereby a person's talents and yearnings propel him to
achieve success in the entire solar system planetary domain.
He is hailed by diverse denizens and life forms while
maintaining his home and connections on planet Earth.

However,
if a person would practice meditation on the first and
second matra of OM,
then in the mind a wondrous blossoming occurs.

By the hymns of the Yajurveda, the seeker, to the solar
system consisting of the moon and planets rises to.

In the solar system having attained to fame, he again returns
to earth since he maintains attachment to the worldly plane.

Hence he becomes wise to the collective spirit.

He now recognizes fully
the transcendental godly Being deep in the recesses of the
heart in his own sprawling body-City.

OM - its third matra "Mmm"

5.5 Rarely enough, do men seek far bigger workplaces.

By sincerely practicing and meditating in sequence on
- the first matra "Amm" with attention on the
  Manipura Chakra at the Navel,
- the second matra "Umm" with attention on the
  Anahata Chakra at the Heart,
- the third matra "Mmm" with attention on the Ajna
  Chakra between the Eyebrows

the quantum cosmic laws get revealed as described in the
Samaveda. The spirit gets supremely elevated. The farthest
regions of creation open up to welcome. Space, Light,
Sound, Gravity, Time; are all mastered.

Thereby a person's talents and yearnings propel him to
achieve success in the entire solar system planetary domain.
He is hailed by diverse denizens and life forms while
maintaining his home and connections on planet Earth.

Moreover, the one who would likewise practice meditation
on this first, second, and third matra of OM,

by the imperishable transcendental Brahman,
he in the effulgent milky way of the sun becomes provided
for.

Just as a serpent sheds its skin as a normal process,

likewise verily the aspirant drops his mind's baggage of grief, turmoil, conflict and hatred.

By the hymns of the Samaveda = the juice and rhythm in creation,

the devotee's spirit to the galactic domain expands.

That is the essence of this verse which is also elucidated in the next two verses.

OM - its connecting ardha matra

5.6 The proper chanting of OM and by deeply meditating on the sacred sound establishes the ardha matra, or its divinity, that underlies and connects.

It is what shapes our notions and makes the intellect mature. It is which keeps us away from harm.

Saints have taught that AUM consists of A, U, M matras, and the <u>invisible unheard ardha matra</u>, permeating all.

The three matras one at a time, practiced and used, give benefits that are spectacular in the relative SPACE-TIME domain.

When done methodically in sequence,
as learnt properly from a Master
with the body-mind-breath in tandem and well-aligned,
in harmony and with pure intent,

Then the one having knowledge and skill

does not waver from his status, is never tempted to go for distracting pleasures, does not fall from grace.

5.7 By the mastery of Rigveda - this humility of Earth is achieved,
by mastery of Yajurveda – the trust of the Solar System is got,
as known by the learned wise men
by mastery of Samaveda – the freedom to function and travel in the entire Galaxy is gained.

It is Guru Grace that keeps the mind innocent and free of bias - that is the underlying achievement of it all – that is what is really worthy of attainment.

Since that grace bestows:
peaceful acceptance and fortitude in old age situations.

The wise person by the sacred syllable OM by the practice of its techniques and deep meditations, definitely achieves union with the Divine.

---

and full stop. And End of class. The teaching is till here.

6th **Question by Sukeśā**

Who is the Being with 16 attributes?
Of course, Oneself.

Sixteen Attributes of Being

The fully blossomed human being with the 5 elements in
harmony, the 5 vayus functioning smoothly, the 5 senses
turned inward, and the mind merged in the Divine.

6.1 Finally love has smitten. A prince is asking;
the prince who is hoping to fall in love.

Clothing his quest in the number sixteen. Sweet sixteen, an
attraction, the pull of love is hidden in this quest.

Initially we might fall in love with something pretty,
something small, just a toy or a toffee.
Later when the intellect expands and the heart ripens, one
only seeks love within!
(though one may wish for an external confirmation)

- Pain of truth leads to liberation.
- Lack is shockingly painful.
- Not denying the lack sparks the journey for
  fulfillment.

5 Elements+5 Prana Vayu+5 Senses+Mind

What has been studied earlier has been summarized here in
the last question. We have seen in detail the
- five Elements – space, air, light, water, earth
- five Vayus – prana, apana, vyana, samana, udana
- five Senses – sound, touch, sight, taste, smell
- one Mind – that rules all and is ruled by all

6.2 That Being you are seeking, resides within this same
body, whether yours or mine.

To them he (the Master) spoke.
"O Children! here in the body itself the Supreme dwells, in whom these sixteen attributes appear and become still".

6.3 The Being intelligently devised a formula whereby it could stay in peace, and depart at will.

The supreme contemplated –
how may I expanding-expansive become…

likewise how stilling all
a silent stillness –
a point may I be,
thus.

6.4 The formula structure:
Life force to begin with, that gives life
- to emotions e.g., Faith and Trust
- to the elements space, air, light, water, earth
- to the senses
- to the mind and its components
- to the food chain

The food chain helps sustain
- strength and vitality
- routine and discipline
- reading, learning, and media
- works, activity, and engagements
- diverse cultures, races, lands and aliens

The diverse cultures having distinct names, independent personalities, aims and ideals:

He, the vital life force, created from the breath,
intense trust or intimacy or love or willingness for each other,
space, air, light, water, earth,
senses, mind, and food.

Using nourishment He created:
strength and stamina,
hard work and discipline,
tools and methods and techniques,
work, act, endeavor, aim.
universes, galaxies, planes with diverse laws and beings.
And in the universe, names, identities, feelings of mineness and
distinction.

6.5 How the formula works perfectly – an analogy:

Just as all these streams flowing towards the ocean,
having merged with the ocean disappear, obliterate their
individual name and form identities,
The ocean thus only it is then called.

Likewise these sixteen great attributes dissolving in the
Supreme Consciousness disappear,
having merged with the Brahman and
having erased their identities,
Brahman thus alone it is called then.

He, this attributeless, imperishable then becomes.
Further explained in next verse.

Just as many streams, rivers, rivulets, water buckets,
raindrops, and drains too, all flow down to the ocean; and
once there they all lose themselves. Their independent
identity no longer persists. It is all simply Ocean.

Likewise, the senses, elements, pancha prana vayu, bodies, minds, and the rest, whether cosmic dust or living beings, or anything else, when these merge in Brahman the infinite, there is naught else, simply the Infinite Brahman.

6.6 Another analogy to drive the point home.

In a fast-moving chariot, the spokes of the wheel are all a blur, the fan blades become transparent, matter dissolves in thin air.

Likewise, when the movie stops, only the pure white screen remains.

When one realizes the Truth, all dissimilarities, polarities, and grievances fade, death becomes a passing fad.

No longer doth worry haunt, nor fear remain.

Hence make it your foremost priority to delve into the illuminating scriptures at the feet of the Master, so that your life may blossom and you may enjoy great peace and happiness.
Just as spokes in the chariot wheel are well fitted, similarly all divine virtues in which are well ingrained,

that is worth aiming, studying, and attaining,
that Supreme Consciousness you must endeavor for,

may frustration, emptiness, desolateness not your life lay waste.

6.7 The Master sums up:

Long and True has been our Satsang, our association has surely elucidated and revealed the Divine.

Purer than Divinity naught any,
Higher than its attainment no aim.
To them (*with love in his voice)* he concluded -
"this is all completely what regarding THE transcendental

Brahman I know".

"Nothing surpassing beyond it exists.
I conclude here finally".

6.8 The satiated disciples exult gratefully:

O Super Soul!
Thee art surely our beloved parent.
Thee hath cast us beyond all dangers-clutches.
Thee have taken us safely home.

Loving prostrations! Wholehearted obeisance.
The six seekers to the Master devotedly bowed, saying -
Thou art (*quivering with emotion, tears running down their cheeks)* our most respected guardian.
Thou who hath completely shred and cleared our shroud of dense notions, fears, misunderstood concepts and narrow vision, and
Established us in the transcendental loving joyful divinity.
Heartfelt Gratefulness to Thee.

Aren't we all seeking Love?
Prashna ends on this poignant note.

7 The Aitareya Upanishad

Peace Invocation

O Lord!

In my speech, may my awareness be fully present. May I be conscious of my tongue at all times.

Lord please give me your precious time, may I affirm those divine moments when I am at total rest.

May the sacred texts beckon to me and speak to me. May I truly recall, recollect, and apply the wisdom.

May I follow the protocols of society. May I be true to my heart and convictions.

May you protect me and my master, my school and my employer. May my family and environs be safe.

May the one who guides me be fully blessed.

Peace in our heart, in our body and in our environs.

Cast of Characters

BRAHMAN

VIRAT or MAYA

DIVINE ADMINISTRATORS

The discourse giver = Aitareya Rishi
The listener = Devotee = you or me.

<u>Rig Veda = Rigveda Samhita + Rigveda Brahmana</u>

Aitareya is one of the earliest Upanishads and is attributed to sage Mahidasa Aitareya. It consists of five sections, viz. sections 21 to 25. These sections form the 4th, 5th and 6th chapters of the 2nd part of the Rigveda Aranyaka.

As of today the Rigveda Brahmana is available in two recensions named Aitareya and Kauṣitaki, of which the Rigveda Aranyaka is a subset.

For

- the Young student the Samhita verses
- the Householder the Brahmana verses
- the Retired the Aranyaka verses

- the Sannyasi the Upanishad verses.

Young Student = one who is yet being cared for by parents.
Householder = one who is in the thick of earning, raising a family, or actively engaged in society.
Retired = one who is out of the grind and living on savings.
Sannyasi = one who is free in mind and light at heart.

These four phases are not separated in time or by age. These may occur in any order in a man's life, sometimes concurrent, sometimes distinct. One may have the Sannyasa experience earlier and get thrown into the Householder struggle later. It happens. The key point to understand is that these are states of the mind, heart, intellect and emotion, and one's relationships in society.

"Aitareya" means the one whose mother is named Itara. "Mahidasa" means the one who serves Mother Earth. It is said this Upanishad is by Mahidasa Aitareya.

Using simple yet elegant words, the Rishi narrates the story of creation from the Big Bang onwards. The complete paraphernalia for its functioning is described, also the biology of man's birth. An incisive statement is made that points to the undeniable fact "Opposite Values are Complementary in Nature".

Its mahavakya is **prajñānaṃ brahma, i.e. Consciousness = the Divine = the Supreme.**

Giving the example of sage Vamadeva who attained enlightenment, a devotee is inspired and empowered to embark on an inward journey…

aitareyopaniṣad

atha Aitareya Upaniṣad

Now begins Aitareya

None Other

In the forgotten past, in the far unseen beginnings, there was only the lone Atman, the Soul. A thought sprang up seemingly in the Atman, a wish for diversity.

Origin – the Thought

That thoughtful wish gave rise to infinite planes, planes with distinct natural laws, some intersecting, others entirely unrelated.

Infrastructure – the 4 Planes

For our current study, we enumerate four planes
- **ambh**, the plane of dark matter.
- **marīchī**, the plane of light energy.
- **mar**, the plane of cyclic duality.
- **ap**, the plane of hidden currents.

Energy – the Virāt

Then the story goes, another thoughtful wish arose. A desire to have administration. This manifested as Virāt, a massive column of energy.

Administration – the Deities
From the massive energy column burst forth various deities and their associated paraphernalia to govern the infrastructure. Each Deity consisted of
- Indriya, the sensing apparatus.
- Indriyagolak, the housing spaces for the senses.
- Indriya-Adhiṣṭhātā, the chief deity for each sense.

Birth – the Biology
All births were given a threefold Staging.
- Love making.
- Pregnancy.
- Birth.

- Womb embryo.
- Walking talking body.
- Genetic lineage that continued.

- Waking State.
- Dreaming State.
- Deep Sleep State.

Need – the Want

As a natural consequence, each deity got infused with the
need to fulfill itself. It took the shape of a triple longing
- Food.
- Work and Companionship.
- Pleasure and Entertainment.

Fulfillment – the Three

The moment of final reckoning arrived. The needs were
richly satiated, using three principles
- Gau, Cow products to satisfy food.
- Aśva, Horse for work-travel-company.
- Man, for utter unending entertainment.

and in turn arose integration.

Grasping – How to Eat? How to Digest?

The senses failed to grasp. The mind failed to reason.

Glue – the Apana Vayu

When the end-to-end chain of components all got
fashioned, they could not be fitted together. The senses
failed to grasp, the mind failed to reason. Then Glue arose to

integrate them all into an independent functioning unit. It was named Apana Vayu, the binding assimilating breath.

and in turn arose responsibility.

Responsibility – the Balance
Finally, the Lord decided to lend a hand.

The responsibility of shouldering the creation fell squarely on his shoulders, but he decided not to do it openly, so as not to miss the fun, that being his prime motive in starting the whole thing.

Very ingeniously, the Lord made
- Brahmarāndra, invisible orifice in the head, sutures in the skull, for his entry-exit.
- Heart's deep recesses for his resting place.
- Guru Śiṣya parampara and Grace as the means to uniting with Him.

Awakening – the Indra

Consciousness or Soul has been denoted by the varied components within every being
- Heart, the heart filled with love
- Mind, the mind of cheerful innocence
- Knowledge that is unbiased
- Order and Discipline
- Science
- Consciousness
- Intelligence
- Vision and Mission
- Endurance
- Firm opinion

- Free will
- Shyness and coyness
- Memory power
- Determination
- High ideal
- Intense passion
- Sense of strong ownership

Consciousness is in fact every imaginable and unforeseen name and form. Each and everything
- living and non-living;
- animal, tree, human and alien;
- sand, grain, television and vehicle

is the reflection of the Supreme Consciousness.

The entire visible and invisible spectrum is
- Established in the Supreme Consciousness
- InspiredNourished by SupremeConsciousness
- Willed by the Supreme Consciousness

Consciousness is
- Beyond right and wrong
- Beyond logic and senses
- Everything and Nothing simultaneously

Consciousness has been equated to (only for teaching)
- The Sun as all-pervading light
- The Space as the container of all and as unaffected by anything
- The Pure White screen on which a movie is projected

The One who assimilates this knowledge and lives this wisdom
- shakes off all shackles,

- exits from guilt and grief,
- gets firmly established in Advaita,
- ceases to hanker for cravings,
- attains union with the Divine, and
- is known as the Eternally Blissful.

1st *Chapter* 1st *Section*
Leela = the Divine Will

In the timeless beginnings this one Soul alone was there. None other was seen. And it "the worlds let me create" thus thought.

1.1.1 Before the beginning only the one Brahman existed. There was naught else. Brahman willed – "**Let me create Planes of Play**". In Sanskrit the term is Leela = the Divine Play.

Origin or Big Bang has been visualized by the ancient Seers as a 3-step matrix, with an underlying 4th facet.
1. Consciousness a perfect Stillness.
2. Consciousness projects a single Entity, its power known as Virat or Maya.
3. Conscious Projection differentiates into infinite planes, worlds, universes, intelligences, elements, energies, timeframes.

This matrix has the underlying facet that the Consciousness and its Conscious Projection display a sinusoidal character,

- exhibiting, dissolving – manifest, unmanifest. This facet is reflected as the duality in creation in all aspects.

It is known as the first law to be taught, studied, ingrained and learnt; to lead a happy life.

Opposite Values are Complementary in Nature
Sri Sri Ravi Shankar

Some things may be perceived as ugly, cruel, or disdainful. No matter, do not stain your heart, act from the intellect as per the norms of society, do not become bitter.

Brahman these worlds created:
- celestial flowing plane,
- luminous planes,
- cyclic plane, and
- underground waters.

that
farthest celestial vaporous fluidic plane with sky as support,
the interstellar galactic planes,
the solar system of cyclic nature, and
the underground waters nearer than the rest.

1.1.2 Planes of Existence

By Brahman's willing, many diverse planes of existence sprouted. The Principal four planes are mentioned to account for infinity.

- Ambhas = Dark Matter and Energy = Black Hole

- Marichi = Stellar Dust & Galaxies = Star Systems

-     Mar = Cyclical = Planetary Systems
-     Aap = Subterranean Waters = Hidden Emotion

Notice that

-     "Ambhas" is neuter by definition
-     "Marichi" is feminine by definition
-     "Mar" is masculine by definition
-     "Aap" again feminine since that gives birth

Diverse meaning separated and distinct in terms of natural laws, governing principles, life forms, modes of intelligence, concepts of right and wrong, definitions of essential and redundant.

Brahman then contemplated "for these worlds administrators verily let me create" thus.

Brahman, from the waters as if popped up instantaneously, a figure fashioned.

1.1.3 Law and Governance

Typical planes are

Ambhas = plane of dark viscous fluids and gluey wetness,

Marichi = plane of lights and brilliant intellect.

Mar = plane of cyclical adventures,

Aap = plane of deepset emotions and their outburst.

To house these planes and make them functional and their laws non-intersecting, the space was seemingly divided into

- black matter or black holes with no identifiable phenomena
- galactic matter with luminous bodies and measurable activity
- solar systems with cyclic seasons, cyclic habitation, cyclic birth.
- worlds which preferred to be hidden, mysterious phenomena that couldn't be explained, couldn't be relied upon, couldn't be replicated.

Then the Divine willed Governance, and it took the shape of a massive human body. The "human body" is just an after thought. We can more accurately say a huge figure that covered the entire space housing the three "Marichi", "Mar" and "Aap" planes.

The rest of this Upanishad teaching leaves out the "Ambhas" plane of dark matter.

1.1.4 Deities for Administration.

Now that infrastructure is done, let me make principles for rulership and efficient governance.

Lo and Behold, subConsciousness or the power of Brahman was thus born. It gave rise to
mouth that gave rise to expression that gave rise to heat. The expression became modulated as speech, while heat got the body of fire.
nose that gave rise to sensing that gave rise to the life force that gave rise to air. Sensing became modulated as smell

and intuition. The **life force** became the unit of life and air became the mechanism of carrying the life force.

eyes that gave rise to sight that gave rise to the light. Sight became modulated as vision and clear thought, and light got housed in the body of the Sun.

ears that gave rise to sound that expanded as space.

skin that gave rise to fine strands that gave rise to grass, herb, tree.

heart that created the mind that gave rise to waxing and waning. The mind housed thoughts and emotions which were always in a flux, thereby the moon was fashioned to substantiate the mind's modulations.

navel that gave rise to a gut that was prone to aging and dissolution.

genitals that gave birth to new seed that needed fertile fluids to propagate. The fertile fluids got housed in a body of water.

He the massive figure deeply meditated. Of his deep penance a face popped up just like a fertilized egg. From that face

- Speech, and from speech heat, got produced.
- Two nostrils popped out, from nostrils the life breath, from life breath the Air.
- Two eyes popped out, from eyes vision, from vision the Sun.
- Two ears popped out, from ears hearing, from hearing the four corners.
- Skin mushroomed, from skin hair, from hair herbs and vegetables.
- Heart opened up, from heart the mind, from mind the moon.
- Solar Plexus Navel popped up, from navel the Apana Digestive Breath, from Apana Vayu the Exit.

- Phallus shot up, from phallus the seed, from seed waters and fluids manifested.

The 3 aspects of Brahman

We have seen the three aspects of Brahman as
- Unqualified undifferentiated Brahman
- Maya = a Power of Brahman
- Principal Features of Maya viz. Senses, AntahKarana, Digestion & Exit

Qualifications for an aspirant

Traditionally, each seeker is advised to perfect these traits so that the Upanishad can be properly understood, practiced, and assimilated.

sādhana–catuṣṭaya the 4 personality traits made by intense satvic effort:

1) Trusting, discriminating attitude. Viveka.

2) Dispassion or restraint in matters unconnected to job. Not overstepping one's domain. Vairagya.

3) Willingness and endurance to persevere for a length of time, e.g. a year. Shat Sampatti.

4) A desire to learn, evolve, become more useful. Mumukshutva.

1st Chapter 2nd Section

Leela = Divine's Subtle Domain

Those referred to earlier, the manifested divine administrators, from this great ocean spreading out fell. He, the Virat = Mammoth figure - with hunger and thirst was infused.

The divine administrators to Brahman pleaded "for us space/territory please indicate wherein being well established nourishment we may get", thus.

1.2.1 Nourishment

Now that the infrastructure and the governing principles having been fashioned, a strong need was felt to feast, enjoy and entertain.

For the Divine Leela to proceed, a mechanism was willed by Brahman. This mechanism is known as need for
- Food
- Company
- Pleasure

for the divine administrators the figure of a cow was displayed. they responded "this certainly for us is not sufficient", thus.
for them, a horse was brought. they reacted "this certainly for us is not good enough", thus.

1.2.2 Cow, Horse

This Need took the form of a devotee and prayed. The prayer was answered in stages. The first need of hunger was satisfied by the manifestation of the Cow, source of milk and all delicious sweetmeats.

The adjunct need of social company was fulfilled by the manifestation of the Horse, source of speedy travel to distant lands, and an understanding companion to boot.

Finally the desire for entertainment was also satiated, by the superb construction of a human being. With its thoroughly unpredictable nature, huge craving for pleasure and comfort, vast ingenuity and adaptability, a human being became the perfect toy for the creator's undiluted entertainment.

Cow Horse Human = Food Company Pleasure

So we see, a cow is the principal source of all food items. Cow represents Milk = mother's milk and Ghee or clarified butter and Cowdung the farm fertilizer.

A horse is the perfect companion. It represents society for work and cultural activity and a partner for close comradeship.

Human Being is here alluded to as a pleasure giving element.

for the deities the figure of a human being was fetched. they exulted, "beautifully done! excellent!", thus.
the human form truly is magnificently done.

to the administrators Brahman said, "each your respective place you may take", thus.

1.2.3 Human and the Placements

Correct Placement and Seating as per ability ensures holistic growth and proper nourishment.

Now all the natural forces took their respective places in the body of a being. The deity of sight, the deity of sound, and the other Shaktis got themselves established.

Once the role of an individual is clearly allocated, he can start performance of duty to his optimal capacity. Responsibility whether at work or at home can be fully shouldered when the framework is well-defined and the role is cleanly allocated.

- The deity Heat, speech having become, in the mouth got stationed.
- The deity Air prana having become, both nostrils it activated.
- The Sun eye having made, the eyes energized.
- The Four Quarters hearing having become, two ears impregnated.
- The Herbs and vegetables hair having become, skin made.
- The Moon mind having made, entered the heart.
- Final Exit Apana vayu having become, the Navel Center irradiated.
- The Waters seed having fashioned, the linga phallus moved into.

1.2.4 The functional Matrix

An outline of the geometry and anatomy of the Deities functioning within an individual is stated.

Lord of governing Deity		Purpose	Anatomy
Agni	Heat	Speech = Expression	Mouth
Vayu	Air	Breath = Life	Nostrils
Aditya	Light	Vision = Plan, Aim	Eyes
Disha	Space	Hearing = Coordinates, Limits, Alertness	Ears
Aushadhi	Flora	Hair = Universality, Nourishment, Appearance	Skin
Chandra	Mind	Antahkarna = Thought, Emotion, Bank Balance	Heart
Mrityu	Exit	Apana Vayu = Digestion	Navel
Aapaḥ	Seed	Procreation = Joy, Continuity	Phallus

Then the pair of greed and sadness to Brahman queried, "for us both kindly specify a dwelling place".

To that pair Brahman replied, "both of you amongst all these deities equitably divide, in all of them, proportionate sharing for you two I make". *(this statement is repeated to indicate to the discerning that both good-& bad have shortcomings, both likes & dislikes need to be shed on the path).*

Hence for whichever trait excess is offered, a due portion of that excessiveness, hunger and sadness is.

1.2.5 Greed and Sadness = Need and Longing

No play is complete without opposing tendencies. These forces keep the fun and uncertainty alive and the play going for long.

The deities of Hunger and Thirst also begged to be accommodated. These forces asked the great Lord regarding the mechanism for their manifestation and support.

To their plea the kind Lord asserted - may you take your lodging and boarding in human beings only, and particularly those that fail to be disciplined, have scant regard for others' welfare, and are apt to skip contributing to the state coffers.

The Upanishad hints at all inclusiveness of the human personality.

1st Chapter 3rd Section

Leela = the Divine loves Anonymity

Brahman thought,
 "now for these worlds and governors,
modes of sustenance for them let me manifest".

1.3.1 A Design that takes care of everything is called holistic design.

In each product or gadget, the design and planning must follow the principles enumerated herein.

Now the Supreme Divinity willed the ultimate product for the Leela – **to keep the Act in continuous Play**.

The final product = FOOD, NEED, WANT, DESIRE.

Brahman willed waters by deep contemplation,
thereupon waters appeared,
and
from those waters a physical form took shape.

Wonder of wonders! the form that so materialized,
Food it was.

1.3.2 Lots of meditative thinking, paperwork, scratch pad, thinktank, is what aids research and development.

Without serious thought, integrity of product cannot be established. Without proper aesthetics even the best design falls short.
"Waters" signify the fluid framework for
- love to blossom,
- emotions to be nurtured,
- thought to manifest.

After the framework is ready, a concrete form can materialize.

From that Virat Mammoth figure wishing for nourishment, this created entity, the **Food**, turning away speedily wished to flee.

By tongue that **Food** was wished to be partaken of, however the tongue alone was incompetent to grasp the **Food**.

Because this **Food**, he the Virat figure by lip-expression if could grasp, just sweet-talk would have taken care of the need for nourishment.

1.3.3 Initially there is the stage of beta testing before any product launch.

By word-of-mouth developers are initially contacted. However, word of mouth is not enough.

For a meeting and a plan, initially a call goes through, however just a phone call will never make it a success.

Needs are not completely satisfied by Speech.

By breath that **Food** was wished to be partaken of, however the breath alone was insufficient to grasp the **Food**.

Because this **Food**, if he the Virat by breath could grasp, just a deep breath would have satisfied the demand for nourishment.

1.3.4 And then other methods are added. After an initial phone call, a sense of urgency is infused in the message.

However even that falls short.

Needs are not completely met by Urgency, fast breathing, or deep breath.

By vision that Food was wished to be partaken of, however vision alone was incompetent in grasping Food. Because this Food, if he the Virat by vision could grasp, just having sharp eyesight and looking at beauty would have satisfied the need for nourishment.

1.3.5 Display posters, pamphlets, and eye-catching advertisements are next made and circulated.

Even then success is not guaranteed.

Needs are not fulfilled by idealistic statements alone.

By hearing that Food was wished to be partaken of, however only by alertness the food couldn't be grasped.

Because this Food, if he the Virat by alertness alone could have grasped, just being alert would have met the need for nourishment.

1.3.6 Plays, stage shows, movies, podcasts and radio talk shows are also employed.

We are getting close, but more is necessary.

Needs are not completely satisfied by Alertness and acute listening.

By touch that Food was wished to be seized, however only

by close proximity the Food couldn't be seized.

Because this want, if he the Virat by close proximity could have seized,
Just being together the want for nourishment would have satiated.

1.3.7 Close contact is made. Physical touch is employed. Personal visits are arranged.

It is still not enough.

Needs are not completely satisfied by Touch or Embrace.

By intelligence that hunger was wished to be fulfilled,
however intellect alone couldn't suppress the hunger.

Because this hunger, if he the Virat by astute thinking and memory could fulfill,
just thinking and contemplating would have resolved the hunger.

1.3.8 Debates are arranged. Discourses are given by renowned orators. Legal attorneys are hired to establish the point.

Still short of the goal.

Needs are not completely satisfied by smartness alone.

By the phallus that **Need** was wished to be fulfilled,

however by intercourse alone the **Need** certainly was not fulfilled.

Because this **Need**, if he the Virat by love-making could have fulfilled,
just by dispensing one's seed, all **Wants** would have been satiated.

1.3.9 The matter of intimacy is resorted to. Sweetened offers are made. Promises are backed up with juicy perks and privileges.

Something is still amiss.

Needs are not wholly met by Love-making.

That **Desire** by the Apana vayu was wished to be assimilated,
And lo and behold! Desire got consummated.

260 Aitareya

Thus, of **Food-Need-Want-Desire**, the Deity Apana Vayu is
the consumer,

the Outgoing breath which digests and assimilates all **Food**
and **Thought** and **Want**,
indeed, is the principal force.

1.3.10 Finally, the method of integration of the complete
chain (so far tried in bits and pieces) is employed.

Success.

End-to-end Integration is the key for great success in any
venture.

The Apana Vayu or the Digestive Breath is the key to food
assimilation and desire fulfillment. It helps to digest
thoughts and emotions and knotty issues as well.

Many Yogic methods, Asana, Pranayama and Meditation are
practiced to maintain a healthy Apana Vayu.

Dharana Dhyana Samadhi helps achieve a very stable Apana
Vayu.

Brahman reflected "now how this body-Mind thing can
porperly function without my conscious presence?"

He the Supreme contemplated "by what means may I enter this gadget?"

1.3.11 The pure exit and reentry is finally planned.

Backwards integration with earlier versions, and keeping in mind future developments and long-term viability, the design now incorporates an active reusability mechanism.

The Lord at last figures out that he must fit into the entire scheme of creation, since without his conscious presence it is all just a lifeless mass.

The Lord pondered,

"if by the Deity Speech alone expression is possible,
if by the Life force alone life is infused,
if by the Deity Sight alone vision is possible,
if by the Deity Sound alone hearing,
if by the Deity Touch alone close contact,
if by the Deity Mind alone thinking,
if by the Deity Apana Vayu alone digestion and assimilation and strength,
if by the Deity Phallus alone further creation,

then what would be my role? My need?
Then I would be completely redundant isn't it"!

He the great Soul, as if the sutures on the skull having cut, by this door entered.
This door is named Vidriti = openable or known by special technique alone.

It is blissful. (being able to reach this doorway, as yogis do in meditation).

Of the Soul's three resting places, three states of equilibrium are envisioned, namely this place and state, that place and state, and also the third place.

1.3.12 The safeguard to prevent accidental use and infringement is tabled. A nondescript and out of the limelight method is put in place. This ensures well-being, happiness, and relative peace of mind to the owner.

For the human Consciousness,
The three places within the body where it dwells are (1) senses (2) intellect (3) heart, without a doubt.
Its corresponding three states of presence (i) while waking in the senses (ii) while dreaming in the intellect (iii) while deep sleeping in the heart.

"Three Places Present" this esoteric term in the Upanishad can also be interpreted as the three distinct phases of a human being

(a) foetus in the mother's womb

(b) life as one's stature in society

(c) known through father or son or family tree whomsoever society closely identifies a person with.

Consciousness of each individual is bigger than the Body. For an analogy consider the Consciousness to be the flame and the Body to be the wick of a candle.

The **twinkle** in one's eye is the presence of consciousness. Similarly the fine **opinion** in the intellect and the powerful

emotion in the heart are the reflections of one's consciousness.

Brahman who finally got born as the embodied beings and became the trapped Soul within, contemplated:

"here what is that which is worth"?
In answer,
"the undifferentiated Brahman as the source of the embodied human soul" it perceived.
And proclaimed with lasting finality "IT (the Brahman) I (the seeker) have experienced", thus. (इति ३)

Notice the *pluta vowel* in the Upanishad verse. It is the mark of deep contemplation. Long silent meditation.

1.3.13 The Transcendent loves mystery.

The noble person remains out of the glare of society. The saint prefers not to reveal his powers to all.

Anything divine, anything sacred assumes the power of secrecy. It becomes hidden. It is never directly disclosed. It is not in public view. It cannot be common knowledge.

Then what is the answer? How can it be realized?
In Deep Meditation. By Dharana Dhyana Samadhi the seeker experiences the Divine.
- Dharana – a focus or contraction.
- Dhyana – letting go or expansion.
- Samadhi – deep restful meditation.

He gets a lasting vision of the ultimate reality. He proclaims it to himself. He announces not to the world outside, but to himself alone. This is not a verbal proclamation. It is simply an affirmation and assimilation deep inside the heart.

Patanjali Yoga Sutras. The Sanyam Course of the Art of Living Foundation.

Hence this-inward-seeing entity,
Indeed Turned-Inward its name.

A seeker on being Meditative, "I am Indra", thus in deep meditation visualizes.

The gods favor Deep Contemplation alone,
the Divine Deities prefer anonymity, hence are beyond the grasp of senses, and cannot be proved nor disproved by logic.

Senses Turned Inward = Sight lowered at angle of 30°.
Famous meditative posture of Gautama Buddha.

1.3.14 It has been the experience of all sages down the ages.

Controlling one's senses = Brahmacharya is a primary step for a sadhaka to attain final liberation.

Lord is invisible. Lord is beyond rhyme and reason.

Consciousness has been called by the names
- Brahman = Vast, the infinite
- Indra = Senses Overlord, the balancer
- Prajapati = Emperor, the topmost ruler
- Devi–Devata = Talents, the skills that give joy
- Panca maha bhuta = Physics Chemistry Math

Consciousness takes birth by the routes
- Embryonic Womb of a mating
- Heat in the Sweat produced by hard effort
- Egg of a mating
- Shoot of a plant

2nd Chapter 1st Section

The Story becomes Personal hence Real

So far, we had opened our aperture wide, very wide. We took a bite of TIME SPACE with both arms.

Now we zoom and focus. We put the limelight on ourselves. We point a straight finger. Inwards.

2.1.1 Genetics

In the body of man is *(spoken with seriousness and earnestness)* this initial embryo.
What this sperm does is that from all organs it the vitality properly collects and bears in its central core the packet of emotions and desires.

The sperm when in the female is inserted then it procreates, that of life is the common birth.
Common birth is one that is familiar to all.

We know the normal mechanism of love-making and reproduction.

What this verse adds is that the bundle of emotions-sensations-ambitions-convictions, all of it apart from the physical traits,

is also in the design blueprint of new birth.

A short course on genetic engineering.

2.1.2 Responsibility of Intimacy is Total
That sperm into the lady an intimate part becomes.
Just as her own body part and emotion.
Hence to her doesn't cause any harm.
She of it like her own self treats, and thereby nurtures.

Of intimacy it is said, it becomes owned, it becomes very close, so dear that it is nurtured, taken care of exceedingly well.

Whatever one assumes ownership of, the responsibility taken for that is total.

2.1.3 Specially Born to continue Legacy
She the one carrying the baby herself becomes the one who is to be exceptionally well taken care of. That lady nurtures the embryo.

The father also till the time of delivery, of the child in the womb, before and after birth takes remarkable care. The father of that child prior and post-delivery gives proper attention.

The father of that child,
 prior and post-delivery,
 gives proper attention to detail.

Based on which talents are desirable,
- He accordingly maintains himself.
- He creates a suitable atmosphere for the pregnant mother.
- Both give particular attention to foods eaten, movies watched, songs played, conversations done.
- Yoga, Pranayama, soothing music, and reading and chanting of scriptures are especially favored.

As one's own self the child is reared, for continuity of the bloodline, in all regions and cultures.

Likewise the continuity of the lineage in these lands and peoples, that of Life is the special birth.

2.1.4 The Undying Birth

Man in the form of Father and Mother, having done the job of giving birth and rearing, their child-Soul now turns towards meritorious and noble deeds.

In due course of time the child having grown into adulthood, and his physical body having fulfilled all responsibilities, duly departs, ripened in old age.

Man dropping this body forthwith is reborn. Verily that of Life is the undying birth.

The soul travels through bodies. It also travels through traits and virtues.

Since a Soul gets known and remembered in diverse ways
- Through physical lineage
- Through propagation of ideals
- Through celebration of festivals and anniversaries
- Some other means

Hence it is known as the Undying Birth.

2.1.5 Vāmadeva Ṛṣi's Blessing
Quote of a famous Sage,

"Myself having been in womb(s)
and having minutely known these
godly births nay worldly times,
in a hundred cityBodies,
ironlike protection nay imprison,
Myself hawk-like in the twinkling of an eye rent it asunder".

This is the story of an enlightened Master. Its revelation has the power to release a human being's bonds.

It is a verse of great impact.
It has liberated many souls.

As if resting in the womb, so the story goes, the great Rishi Vamadeva thus affirmed.

2.1.6 is a tour de force
and for all seekers a lighthouse.

He, Vamadeva achieving this wisdom,
from this body getting liberated,
rising beyond the gravity of the mortal plane,
to the blissful heavenly plane,
all plans having exhausted,
the nectar gained.

He became united with the Eternal.

How to be liberated? - By Letting Go. A recap of Origin,
Infrastructure, Administration, Deities, Nourishment. Finally
the Lord surveyed his handiwork. Something seems to be
amiss he felt. "There should be a basic theme - a certain
principle - that when applied would make it all meaningful
to a discerning individual. Would establish him in dynamic
harmony. Would give him a glimpse of deep peace. Of Bliss.
Freedom. Nirvana".

The ultimate beauty, the most precious love, the supremely
desirable was not to be had by any of the senses. Not by
sight, nor smell, nor hearing, nor taste, nor touch. Neither
was it had by the intellect, nor by indulgence in procreation,
nor by force of strength. Certainly not by plunging to death
or engaging in injury to body or self.

By a grace and practice that energized the sahasrara chakra
could the Brahman be united with. Could ultimate
happiness result. However, that couldn't be everyone's call.
For everyone the Deep Sleep attribute was willed to give

rest, a sense of peace, bliss, freedom. And this Shakti came to be called Indra - pacifier of mind and senses - giver of hope, and love, yet mysterious since sleep couldn't be brought on by will nor could it be denied if it came.

3rd Chapter 1st Section

Freedom Mukti Nirvana

Contemplation and Deep Meditation lead man home.

3.1.1 In Peace, Man begins to Reflect

"Who and What is this Soul?" *quote*

that we all with so much sincerity seek, contemplate, and meditate upon.

Which of the two is the actual Soul?
by which sees or
by which hears or
by which fragrances smells or
by which speech articulates or
by which the tasty and the bland especially knows?

Man gets a moment of peace. The ambient stillness and the lack of active to-do lists, cause something Beautiful to happen.

When the external environment is calm, and the inner thought is peaceful, then the Magic happens.

Contemplation on the Supreme Divinity arises. Interest in the Bigness awakens.

3.1.2 All Noble Qualities are Its Reflection

Now we see the whole gamut of noble virtues and qualities as being a reflection of the Supreme alone.
What rules the Heart, the same governs the Mind as well.

It is proper knowledge, orderly knowledge, scientific knowledge, awakened knowledge,

also the same expresses as intelligence, insight, perseverance, sound opinion, freedom of thought, shyness, clear memory, strong decision, earnestness, quiver-free breath, to have and own the desirable etc.

All these indeed
of the Consciousness
various names are.

3.1.3 prajñānaṃ brahma

prajñānaṃ brahma
Consciousness = Brahman.
Life = Divine.
Living = Respectable.

A *Mahavakya* - verse of supreme understanding. An Enlightened statement.

This me within
is Brahma = the Vast Infinity,
is Indra = Lord of Senses,

is Prajapati = the Lord of all Beings.

It is all these deities = skills and talents.
And it is the five great elements –
Earth, Air, Space, Water, and the Light.
It is like a judicious mix of many small things, various virtues
and attributes. It covers the spectrum of all insignificant
creatures like bacteria and virus, ant and scorpion.

Whether born of seed, or else of egg, or womb, or sweat-
produced-warmth, or shoot

in various bodies, e.g. Horses, Cows, Humans, Elephants.

Whatever that breathes, has feet, has wing, and whatever
immobile;

all that is Consciousness-Led. Willed by the Supreme.
In consciousness rooted, a consciously-dictated world
consciously supported. Consciousness = Brahman.

prajñānaṃ brahma - A MAHAVAKYA
prajñā = Awareness = the Lord.
prajñā = Consciousness = Brahman.

3.1.4 O! Such fabulous wealth

He by this conscious soul from this worldly-struggles-plane having broken free,

in this heavenly blissful plane all aims having been fulfilled and taken care of,

duly attains immortality.

Man became fully immortal, all pervasive, reposed in the Self.

What a joy to behold the nectar within.
What blissful charm to be acquainted with the inner strength.

What greatness can equal the purity and humility of the Soul of Man?

Such a treasure. O! Such fabulous wealth.

Indeed fortunate is the man who glimpses his inner space.
The space that is divine, whole, and without lack. The part of him that is God, Godly, Godliness.

We are all Conscious.
We are all a reflection of the Supreme Consciousness.
We are all Brahman.
i.e.
We are all Eternal, Imperishable, Blissful, Divine.

Aitareya ends on this decisive happy note.

8 The Shvetashvatara Upanishad

Peace Invocation

oṃ saha nāvavatu | saha nau bhunaktu | saha vīryaṃ
karavāvahai | tejasvi nāvadhītamastu mā vidviṣāvahai ||
oṃ śānti śānti śāntiḥ ||

O Pure Loving Grace!

May we be taken care of along with family and friends.
May we enjoy socializing, eating, and outing together.
May we support each other's vision and growth and May our
intellect be open to new ideas and changing trends.
May we spend more time in grateful praises, and May we
discuss virtues rather than harp on vices.
Peace in our heart, in our body, and in our environs.

<u>Yajur Veda = Yajurveda Samhita + Yajurveda Brahmana</u>

Shvetashvatara verses are found in the Krishna Yajurveda. There is ample discussion about Brahman, the Supreme Reality, and its manifest transactional play.

śvetāśvataropaniṣad
atha śvetāśvatara upaniṣad

Now the Shvetashvatara

1ˢᵗ Teaching (the brainstorming)

What is Brahman?

Who has the final say?

1.1 Seekers of the Truth (that is deeper and more significant than that evident from sight and hearing) are having a brain storming session.

What is the meaning of Brahman? Why this creation and to what purpose? By whose will does Life get impregnated in matter? Where do we come from where do we go? What happens to us after we leave this earthly plane?

O knower of Brahman, By whose will operate the laws of Pain and pleasure that play havoc on each individual and also give solace?

1.2 who wields more authority and has the final say? Whether wheel of Time, Seasonal changes and cyclical forces, personal necessities, one's attitude and level of understanding, pure coincidence, or the interplay of basic elements and their laws, some known, some undiscovered, some not understood.

We opine none of these listed are the real agencies, how can they be when they themselves seem so fragile, prone to error, unstable?

Nay even the innermost being inside of us is so dim that it seems to be easily overwhelmed and at a loss when faced with trying circumstances, unpleasantness, or wickedness.

O please answer 'who causes the pleasure and pain, who induces love and bondage, who wields final say'?

1.3 after a long time, through persistent discipline and thorough brain storming, the minds became still. Thought waves stopped. It is then that the clouds of emotions parted, deep-set dusty memories got erased, oscillatory thought beams were lifted, and the source was revealed.

It also became apparent that the dense fog of collective emotions memories thoughts was a perfect barrier that kept the source unnoticed, unsought, un-aimed for, as if non-existent.

This veiled entity was then the
Source, the Object of their study, the target of their integrated efforts. It became clear that something that lay hidden beyond the impenetrable mantle of emotionMemoryThought was both the key and the foundation. It was what willed over time and timelessness, it

was what gave form to space, names to individuals and infused life and desire in all.

1.4 Those brilliant students then framed mathematical equations for their conclusions. Their hypothesis after extensive cross-checking and collective note comparing gave birth to a physical prototype.

It was agreed that the Source could be considered of as having a crystalline structure consisting of an outer illuminated circle that spanned the entire 360 degree visible spectrum. The first theorem proved was that the Source had complete access in each direction. It knew, sensed, or could foresee each plan, each motive, and everyone's deepest longing. Then the second theorem proved was that the Source had total control over each outcome, phenomenon, construct whether imaginary or physical.

So a model prototype was drawn on paper and then given shape using steel, wood, glass, clay, paint and ceramic.

This illuminated circle projected triple beams of laser like intensity to reach out and rule over its domain. It was also simultaneously apparent that the Source Control had some stark differences wrt modern control and combat strategies. 1. The Source was equally at ease and retained its fullness and cheerful enthusiasm irrespective of whether its diktat was followed, opposed, or not followed. The controlling beams were tuned to allow equal probability for success, failure, and the impossible.

Each energy beam could be further differentiated into sixteen composite waves. Sixteen is technically the accepted year for love making or explosive virility. Sixteen is technically the age of manhood or womanliness. Most humans reach body proportion, comeliness, and decision-making maturity, hence in class XI a student gets to choose his stream for university graduation, opposite sex dating, and coronation.

Thus, each energy beam had sixteen modules, to account for and allow 1. Hope 2. Fear 3. Passion 4. Sloth 5. Justice 6. Cruelty 7. Merit 8. Hypocrisy 9. Hardness 10. Sublimity 11. To 16. Reserved for each man and animal, each matter particle, each energy and wave to specify their own favorite attribute.

When we say each beam has sixteen concurrent channels, we mean that the energy beam has reached limiting magnitude or has attained terminal velocity, so that its target is easy pie. Its purpose fulfillment is guaranteed.

The Math also lays great stress on the number 20, as our Brahman prototype is thought of as not possible of unveiling unless we do effort of a 20-minute meditation, or a 20 strokes bhastrika, or an education process that moves us to age 20 (class 12+3years of graduation).

Many common animals like dogs, cats, sheep, and cows, all live to a ripe age of twenty. Many sportsmen and world-famous personalities give a glimpse of their talent at this age.

6x8 = 48, this number was introduced to specify six milestones in life. Birth Growth Turbulence Repair Success Dissolution. These six parameters mark the journey of each thing and being, whether living or non-living. Each parameter has a specific period and position.

Eight means the 8 fundamental bodies. Viz.
<u>8 fundamental particles.</u> String Quark Meson Electron Proton Neutron Atom Molecule.
<u>8 fundamental tissues.</u> Bone, bone marrow, blood, plasma, lymphatic fluids, muscle, fat, nerves.
<u>8 fundamental nutritions.</u> Protein, vitamin, fibre, fat, carbohydrate, mineral, water, sunlight.
<u>8 fundamental forces.</u> Gravity, light, magnetism, acceleration, electricity, centrifugal, heat, entropy.

(Source was later christened Brahman, triple beams got named Sattva Rajas Tamas.)

Now the theorem proposed and verified pertained to whether Brahman needed many energies and many devices and many processes to oversee and lord over this infinite spectacle. The prototype said only a single fiber emanating from Brahman attended to each and everything and being, situation and emotion, black hole and galaxy. Unlike the sun that fires a million rays, only one ray from Brahman processed, inspired, subjugated or elevated each and every known and unknown particle and energy, man, beast, gadget, storm, lightening, fusion, fission, waywardness, responsibility, or love.

As if by magic the prototype made a mirror image, depicting the twosome - boys and girls, cold and hot, rage and romance, black and white. Using imperceptible design, Brahman gave a reasoning mind and an emotional heart, those who failed to balance the two were termed normal status quo who would dissolve after 400 years, those who achieved equilibrium achieved unity and lived the remaining years as a jivan mukta, enlightened and free, content and complete.

To further validate this prototype, a test group of 100 scientists was divided into two, one set looked at one prototype from various angles and went into deep contemplation, the other group studied the other prototype and ran various experiments. In the end the data of both groups of 50 scientists was tabled, and a perfect match was found, thus was accepted by all the supremacy of Brahman, and the theorems went into print as fundamental ideas.

1.5 For other sincere seekers, or later to come scientists and saints, a five-fold methodology was made the benchmark. Pancakosha meditation formed the basis as taught by Sri Sri Ravi Shankar in the Happiness program. By this meditation, a man could hope to grasp the essence and embark on the path of Truth.

Even young children could be taught to identify the five basic senses and their importance, and be inspired to take good care of their eyes and teeth and ears and tongue.

Even people who worked very hard and had difficulty in balancing time or making both ends meet could be induced to go for panchakarma sessions for peak performance at work and play.

Scientists and Pioneers could be taught in detail the laws pertaining to the five great elements, so that they could come up with pragmatic inventions and fantastic discoveries.

Spiritual seekers could learn about the five modulations of the thoughts - proof, sleep, memory, inference, fertile imagination and thus stay on the path.

Businessmen, Administrators and defense forces could learn how to use the 5 weaknesses - anger, lust, vanity, infatuation, righteousness to their advantage.

Doctors and Medics would benefit immensely by understanding the five major systems - respiration, circulation, digestion, evacuation,

For Society Civilization and Nation to flourish 50 activities, departments, portfolios were made mandatory.
1 Farming 2 education 3 health 4 defense 5 industry 6 research 7 space 8 ocean 9 mining 10 recycling 11 retail 12 housing 13 roads 14 parks 15 forests 16 wildlife 17 food processing 18 festivities 19 tourism 20 spiritual 21 exercise 22 sports 23 sanitation 24 pregnant mother and newborn 25 religious 26 electricity generation distribution 27 water generation distribution 28 telecom 29 transportation of cargo livestock humans 30 cooking gas generation distribution

1.6 the car and its driver, the mobile phone and its user, the lathe machine and its operator, all aspire to behold Brahman. Sometimes Brahman satisfies the inventor, at other times he blesses the user, and then there are moments when his grace elevates the instrument - the automobile the spoon the tennis ball or the dawg.

Rare is the son who glimpses the divine in his father, many are fathers who sense the Brahman in their offspring. A few cities get a mayor or dc worth his salt, few anyways can't stand him and wish such a noble soul's early exit.

Who is Brahman wonder the sages, in whom is Brahman's current strongest? The theory that he is omnipresent is possibly misapplied, for the sages say Brahman can be omnipresent at will, not that he is there all the time. Likewise Brahman can be omnipotent by choice, not that decides to win every game, or subdue each opponent.

In the end it is agreed by minute study of a large number of events over a large timeSpace continuum that Brahman alone picks the winner, albeit it is found in the majority of cases he picks someone who is sincere dedicated enduring humble and patient.

1.7 On further investigation it is established that Brahman is not at all one-sided, nor does he harbor ill-will, bitterness, frustration or anxiety.

In each being Brahman chooses to play a role, whether the sensuous mind, or the longing heart, or the talented intellect. Sometimes he plays more than one role in a being, in other beings he plays no role at all.

Likewise Brahman may also choose to be the batsman, the bowler or the fielder. He may choose to be a) the pudding b) the act of eating and c) the hungry being. All three at once, one or more of these three, or none at all.

However for sure Brahman is the playground, he is the life, he is the cheering, he is the trophy. Assimilating this fact with a resounding solidarity, the sages got grounded in faith.

This faith became their armor. This faith cleared away all obstacles, this faith made them blissful and divine.

1.8 - 9 A further corollary was added to the thesis. To lay at rest all discrimination and differentiation, it was stated - Brahman himself chose to manifest in differing degrees of radiance.

He manifested along the entire spectrum 0 to 1 and all in between. He manifested in all names and forms from -~ to +~. He made himself superbly intelligent or abysmally dull. Most beautiful or thoroughly unwanted.

Still he ensured that each name and form had some likes at some point in the spaceTime continuum, none went altogether without food, love or friendship.

1.10 - 11 Body is said to be composed of 5 elements that have been blessed to occupy a finite cloud in the timeSpace continuum.

Within this timeSpace cloud, this body is permanent, long lasting and imperishable. Once in specific albeit uncharted moments, Brahman touches this cloud. In other words the Shiva consciousness called "Hara" pulsates and its vibration unites with the timeSpace cloud, though it cannot be established how or when.

The sages can only establish and validate that having distinctly heard these words from the Master, one must become one-pointed in contemplation, again and again seeking to reinforce the Brahman presence. For sure then as if some gates open, as if some dimensions get unlocked, one gets transported to the Brahman plane, merging, uniting, becoming one.

This merging or dissolution or nirvana or enlightenment cannot be sensed by oneself nor by any other self.

There is no outer or visible change, the game continues as before, however instincts like fear, hate, guilt, bitterness, stubbornness bid final adieu.

1.12 by astute discrimination and differentiation One's mind can be separated into three - my desires, desires of my loved one(s), desirelessness.

The student must strive strongly to arrive at this demarcation. Taking copious notes can be of assistance, listening to the words of the Master can be helpful, being in the company of the wise is also fruitful.

1.13 - 14 Another potent technique to arrive in the Brahman space is the sacred syllable Om.

Just as striking a matchstick causes spontaneous birth of fire. But who applies this fact? Only the one who has been so taught and has the proper matchstick. The uninitiated will find it practically impossible to create fire from two pieces of wood.

Analogy of light hidden in wood to suggest Brahman can manifest in any body.

Similarly Om gets infused with radiance only when learnt from the Master, then its assiduous practice brings us so close to Brahman that it reveals itself.

The practice is Sanatan, it can be done variously by various folk. The teaching is also Sanatan, Masters across the continents may teach in any number of ways.

What is common is the commitment, the earnestness, the continuity, and utter lack of righteousness (I right thee wrong).

1.15 - 16 Oil or fluid is a natural ingredient in seeds, but its extraction needs vision, method, planning, hard work and time. Only a few entrepreneurs make the top grade in this regard.

The calves and young of mammals' drink only milk, but man processes the same to produce a plethora of tasty byproducts. Not everyone has the skill to make delicious cottage cheese, or yummy yoghurt, or a mouthwatering rasgulla.

Water of springs and glaciers is highly recommended, however that access is limited to a paltry segment of the population.

Similarly to learn the deepest secrets of the mind, to learn to discriminate and separate layer by layer the bundle of memory and emotion, is not everyone's cup of tea.

Seek out a master who can guide, then serve him and satisfy him to the fullest, it's possible then for Brahman to fall into your lap.

This is the gist of the wisdom that dawned on those brave adventurers who sought out the Truth with exemplary efforts.

2nd Teaching (yogic techniques)

Surya Namaskar

(This chapter lists some practical methods for progressing on the path of yoga).

2.1

To begin with, the aspirant should start with Surya Namaskar, a set of 12 asanas. That quickly strengthens the digestive system, so the senses begin to shed their waywardness.

2.2 the practice can be enhanced with chanting and meditation, and an optimal beginning should include 12 or 24 rounds of Surya Namaskar.

2.3 additionally we can face the eastern direction if possible. In the morning the sunlight is beneficial for the eyes and skin.

2.4 over time one must learn to chant the mantras for each posture, since sound is a powerful modulator of the mind.

2.5 treating the sun as a friend and being grateful for his presence in life is another means of making good progress on the path of yoga. Talk to the sun, allow its rays to touch the entire body for 20 minutes. Especially eyes, nabhi, spine, hands, feet.

2.6 the morning fire ritual known as agnihotra in which two

offerings of ghee are made to a small fire along with invoking the sun deity is also a technique to stabilize oneself on the path of yoga. This ritual needs no initiation, young children can do and feel their eyesight become brighter, the elderly can feel their joints are getting stronger.

2.7 whatever it is, have a place for the sun in your heart. Any which way you can, make the sun worthy of your attention. This technique is also proven to be an asset on the path of yoga.

E.g. sun meditation as guided by Sri Sri Ravi Shankar.
Sun exercises as taught in the Netra Jyoti panchakarma.

2.8 a favorite method involves Keeping the Spine Straight, Torso absolutely still like a statue. Now take your Sahaj Mantra with faint attention in the heart chakra at the center of the chest. Do it cheerfully, without restlessness. If needed play a vigorous game and allow muscles to become warmed, mind to become focused, before attempting this.

2.9 another process involves rhythmic breath as taught by Sri Sri Ravi Shankar in the famed Happiness Course. All the breathing here is through the nose. At the end of the Sudarshan Kriya, ensure that one goes into a relaxed posture for a few minutes, shavasana preferably, so that the Mind can disengage from the senses, the intellect and memory can disconnect from the self, and utter peace is given a chance to correct all imbalances. The shavasana is very much needed to infuse each cell with the nectar generated, don't skip the lying down detox part.

2.10 at a basic level a yoga studio must have even lighting that does not impinge on the eyes, fresh air circulation so enough oxygen levels are maintained, temperate climate control so mind isn't doing unnecessary gymnastics, and clean level flooring of virgin marble or wood.

Gadgets, TV, telephone and other electronic sounds must be avoided so that the inner Om can be heard. Chatter and noises of people talking must be kept to a bare minimum.

It is not recommended to open a yoga studio in a super market or place adjacent to high traffic movement or where babies yell and children squeal.

2.11 During deep meditation, various visions might appear, pay no heed. Do not latch on. Neither block them out, nor engage with them. Do not try to recreate the experience of a session another time.

Each meditation could be different or similar, could have same or disparate effect, just live the experience and move on. Meditation connects to Brahman space, from where one gets to heal one's ancestors as well as descendants, it is hence possible in certain meditative sessions that one feels nothing, since the benefit went to someone else.

2.12 meditations on the 5 elements and the 7 chakras are hugely beneficial.
Such meditations give lasting relief from illness, poor health, mental blocks, and cause a remarkable change in temperament and attitude. 5 elements define our barriers, and transcending each gives immense relief. 7 chakras

define our milestones and achieving these frees our next birth's burden to that extent.

2.13 and how may we know that we are on correct path? There shall be many indications and feedbacks. Among them
- one feels more energetic and enthusiastic, ready for small tasks or gestures which one earlier shirked from.
- common cold, headache, stomach ache frequency drops.
- reduction in lustful tendency
- remarks of Youthfulness from friends or colleagues
- Speech becomes softer, harshness and cruelty of tongue is less
- Body odor becomes imperceptible, sweat no longer bothers
- appetite becomes disciplined, one rarely misses food timing or craves for exotic dishes.

2.14 Glimpses of Brahman become more common, frequently one senses the Lord's presence, heart tastes drops of nectar.

Mind feels clear and less cloudy, there is a dip in fear, frustration, anxiety.

A sense of goodwill prevails.

2.15 The call of the soul is heard. The destiny and design come in focus. Distractions and infatuations disappear.

One's efforts become aligned with the Divine will. Joyousness resurfaces.

2.16 one forgives oneself and slowly learns to forgive others, as the hidden divinity in all become visible.

The deeper layers of consciousness get noticed, the basic building blocks of each being seem more human, friendly, and acceptability increases.

2.17 One becomes friends with the road and with the berm, the lawn and the garden delight our senses, trees becomes precious and sacrosanct.

More efforts are spent in the maintenance of biodiversity and ecology, the rivers and lakes are made clean and fresh, mountains get honored and hiking trails get trekked.

3rd Teaching (deities of Brahman)

Who causes Sleep and Awaking?
Rudra.

3.1 When all men wake up, who wakes them up? When all men sleep who puts them to slumber?
Ponder ponder.

When we see incredible talents blossom in men all over the world, who is responsible for infusing them in the first place?

Is there a Lord of the universe? Is there someone who protects the tender saplings and watches over the babies?

Rare are the folk who wonder and ponder on such inscrutable tracks. Those who so venture on these lonely paths, surely attain the Supreme. They get rid of their frustrations and anxieties, they are elevated to a plane bereft of turmoil.

3.2 There is one fluid that flows in each man. This fluid is the same in each, irrespective of different emotions, currents, and tendencies that are secondary and less important.

The common current in all is not easily perceived, it continues unabated and in full strength, irrespective of circumstances, events, age or any phenomena.

3.3 This fluid Rudra inspires eyes and ears to function, and gives wings to emotions.

Rudra causes notions of heaven and divinity, and also supports the physical planets and galaxies. It remains unaltered in all.

3.4 Rudra is an intelligence that senses all things, all actions, all thoughts, and even unspoken emotions.

Rudra is the force that powers the mighty. It is the prime mover of geniuses.

Rudra creates the golden crucibles that seed every entrepreneur and enterprise.

O blessed force! May our intellect see your core plan and

understand one's native design, may we appreciate your working in each body.

3.5 O Rudra, most auspicious one!
O thee that pervades every body, may the cruelty in us be muted, may our vengeance and rage prove fruitless.

May you enforce calmness in mind and softness in heart. May you throw proper light on the scriptures so that we do not learn them incorrectly.

May you drop down to our level of understanding and aid us in choosing the teaching with simple vocabulary, and thus prevent our intellect from being clouded.

3.6 O the exciter and the cause of virility! Kindly ensure that my energy causes no harm, my action and speech are not misdirected. My aim is true.

3.7 That elusive force within each is hard to perceive, yet is the governor of all great acts.

When we do the exceptional, when the incredible results through us, it is this Supreme current that flows in the creation that gets the credit, not any individual person.

The rare traveller who discerns this eternal hand reaches that plane devoid of sorrow. He is transported to the plane of abundance, where there is no lack.

3.8 O lucky me! I seem to have glimpsed the Supreme Soul, the self-luminous, the one whom darkness does not obscure.

Ignorance only veils thee, it cannot overcome thee.

O lucky me! I feel so comforted and at ease, i feel free. I now move unobstructed and my actions are unthwarted. Methinks only someone who can dig deep within and uncover thee can access the universe's key. Only such a bold and persevering man might taste freedom and live full untainted by regret.

3.9 When we talk of the finer emotion of Rudra like LOVE, we find there isn't anything that stands up to it. Conversely, as LOVE is also soft and weakening, to entice or trap someone there isn't anything better.

When we talk of the fluid nature of Rudra, it becomes apparent that its gigantic waves can knock out an entire galaxy. On the other hand its trickle droplet can seep through the tightest safe and make inroads into the stubborn-nest heart.

Silent motionless too is Rudra, its presence is hence rarely discerned, like a nondescript tree in a forest.

Rudra demands attention from none, it seeks not any company. Stronger than the strongest it cheerfully rests, it feels no need for self-glory.

3.10 Indeed Rudra is in a space unimaginable, its total lack of craving is legendary.

Can you understand this my friend? Can you digest such a

Rudra? Can your heart accept and acknowledge such energy? Can your reason not become a hurdle? If so, then know you are close. You are on track.

Else time hangs heavy, else family and friends seem alien, else work is a drag, and life is a burden.

3.11 In all forms that the eye can see, in all men who walk this planet, know that Rudra is present albeit non-transactable.

All thoughts and all distances are tiny compared to Rudra's domain. His lordly presence and compassionate benevolence are sought for by all, only few make his acquaintance in one lifetime.

3.12 Rudra is hailed by sages as the magnificent indweller of courageous hearts and broad intellects. His light awakens the conscience of man. His presence infuses men with compassion and humility.

3.13 What organ of the body can be used to denote Rudra for purpose of teaching? We can assume the Thumb to represent Rudra, taking into consideration the thumb's size and which can be easily hidden in the fist, its multitasking ability and visible importance.

And where inside the body may we say is Rudra located? It is within one's soul, however since the exact location of the soul is not known, for purpose of teaching we assume it to be in the heart, i.e. the chest center, or the anahata chakra.

How may we know or perceive Rudra?
By a pure heart, by a clarity of intellect, by determined will,
sincere imagination or ardent prayer it can be felt.

Those brave men who strive with priority and urgency to
realize Rudra, attain the superimposition of his will in their
day-to-day life, thus get freed from afflictions.

3.14 One may see and feel Rudra in countless day to day
experiences. a soft sunrise, a brilliant sunset, the leaves
dancing in the breeze.

a loved one's glance, a mother's explosive anger, a
sportsman's exhilaration, a student's exceptional
examination attempt, someone's witty response.

a stroke of lightning, a raging tornado, a burst of lava that
engulfs the town.

Know ye Seeker, Rudra's capability, his ingenuity and
inventiveness, his speed and strength, exceed anything that
has been observed in the 10 directions, or that can be done
by the combined efforts of tens of nations.

3.15 Brahman encompasses Time. What was in the Past,
what is in the Present, what shall be in the Future, are all
within Brahman's preview.

It may appear that parts of him in the form of body and
matter are destructible, and that his energies are
transformable, it is all just his play. Unaffected is he, it is all
just his prank, his style of entertainment are all these names
and forms we see.

3.16 To the devotee, to the bhakta, to the enlightened Master, all the hands that act are doing his bidding, all the feet that walk are walking towards him.

All the beautiful eyes search for him, all the clashing egos announce his pranks, all the handsome faces reflect his glory.

All ears strain to catch his word, all efforts are done to please him alone.

3.17 When senses get purified through the practice of Brahmacharya celibacy, they turn inwards and seek him, they glimpse him and revel in him.

The intellect then acknowledges him as the Boss, the Idol, the Refuge and the best friend.

3.18 The human body has nine exits (2 eyes, 2 ears, nose, mouth, navel, bum, and penis). Each is an entry and exit for Brahman. Each such frame with a capable nervous system can house him and make him welcome.

The pure Swan (an epithet for Brahman as it can separate milk from a watery mix), glides forth and evokes the desire to be free in man. Only men with Viveka and Vairagya discern the graceful Swan or have a glimpse of Brahman.

The rest continue as bound mechanical beings, unduly tied to work and family, overly tied to societal obligations, and never for a moment wish to know Him.

3.19 He has no need for anatomical hands, nor for mechanical feet. His will accomplishes all, by will alone He moves.

Nor does He require sensory eyes or ears or fancy gadgets, His means of information are simply a matter of will.

He can fathom any design and thought, no plans escape His keenness. Only an awakened being can sense Him.

It has been declared by the Enlightened Masters –
"Who came First is He,
Who is a perfect man is He,
Who is Gigantic and Magnificent is He".

3.20 Brahman is fluid and can pass through the smallest atom and influence its spin bypassing any nearby atoms. It can make a single strand of hair lustrous by raising its vitamin levels. It can penetrate deep into the intellect and clear finicky notions.

Brahman is vast and can affect the destiny of entire galactic phenomena. It can infuse any team with the spirit to win the Olympic gold or rule over the World.

A man's heart is the place where it is supposed to be concealed, albeit only in the purer and innocent beings it houses itself.

The brave and the modest are blessed with its grace, the pure souls experience its working, and shorn of covetousness they transcend the plane of heartburn and pain.

3.21 O how fortunate am i to have been blessed by the darshan of the Lord. i feel His presence, i experience His glory, i know He is eternal and that He is my root cause.

i realize He moves in all beings at will, i sense Him in nature and in family, friends, neighbors, also in strangers.

The Sages declare Him to be causeless. The knowers of Brahman declare It to be ever available, always helpful, ready to support the greatest ventures, and lend a hand to the boldest move and the classiest thought.

4th *Teaching (manifest Brahman)*

Necessity of Faith

4.1 He is a well-integrated composite being with innumerable skills at his command. His chief vocation is to create various things and engineer different phenomena. He enjoys a diversity of flora and fauna. He produces various religions, tenets, and dictums, and takes many births to follow and apply one or another practice.

Each practice may be polarized wrt another, each practice may have certain common traits and few vastly different precepts.

May he enlighten the powerful nations so that at least some are able to transcend the differences and revel in the polarity. A melting pot of ideas, a soup of vegetables from far lands, and a mixing of languages and cultures to whom he blesses with, are the most fortunate folk.

4.2 May the powers that be see the same Fire is used for cooking in all homes, and the same Sun at dawn greets all the lands.

The same Air is breathed in and circulated in and out of each nose on the planet.

All men use the same Moon to woo their beloved, all lovers enjoy the one moonlight streaming on earth and romantic Venus to aid their marriages.

The Wisdom in each culture speaks of tolerance, forbearance, sharing and caring.

Waters everywhere quench parched throats and delight the soul.

Farmers Teachers Doctors and Engineers all do the same thing irrespective of language, culture, affiliation or economic status.

4.3 Each Girl and every Boy, whether baby, teen, adult or senior, loves to interact, communicate and exchange.

Excitement erupts on distant meetings of old comrades, friends are thrilled when a long lost face shows up.

Virgins may get involved with oldies, the poor boy may entice the wealthy girl.

It's not a mystery, it's nothing new. Only you the director

pulling the strings and arranging the sets.

4.4 Thou art the blue butterfly, the green hued parrot sporting inquisitive red eyes.

Thou light up the scenery with lightning flashes accompanied with booming thunder from ominous dark clouds.

You cause seasons to unfurl and put up a heroic show every two months, you make the seas teem with millions of salmon, sharks, whales and dolphins.

You cannot be framed in a picture, you cannot be justified by words, it is hard to pinpoint your beginnings if any.

What is sure is that you make us all experience the highest pleasure, you ensure that all beings have their say, their day, and hog the limelight once in a lifetime.

4.5 Uncaused unmade unruled, your energy branches into luminous sattva, energetic rajas, and balancing tamas.

Like a magician's mathematics, the branched energies recombine to produce non-quantifiable, unaccounted for and uncountable beings.

When or how anyone dies or anything destroys is never stated, it seems this is also an incredible law, albeit it satisfies and satiates all.

4.6 O look at myself. Am i not the two, the mind and the soul?

302 Shvetashvatara

Look at my sturdy frame and handsome features, look at my wealth and my beautiful companions.

Q. Who is looking and enjoying all this?
A. Obviously the MIND. The ticking clock in me, the stream of thoughts, the decision maker MIND sitting in the body is experiencing all of it just like a dove sitting on a tree, pecking at berries.

Q. What about the SOUL?
A . O it's calmly watching the spectacle, wondering when the MIND shall look up to it. Certainly that is going to take a long time and many events later only shall the MIND get tired of its shallow living. After it is fully spent, then alone the racing MIND drops and looks up and spots the unperturbed SOUL. Just as the dove looks up and spots its mate only after it's finished with its mundane chore.

4.7 The MIND due to its feverish hankering keeps running hither and tither, then by some grace it gets the SOUL's darshan. One look at the SOUL, one glance by the SOUL, and the MIND understands in a flash that the Captain loves it, the Commander is at its side, the Big Boss is its bosom friend and well-wisher.

In that instant the MIND is freed. In that instant it unites with the SOUL, dropping all pent up emotions, clearing all backlog.

In a flash understanding dawns - the entire creation is for it solely, all wealth in the creation belongs to it alone, there is none but itself there.

This is what Satsang does. Singing together, chanting together, praying together, listening to the Master's discourse, they all lead to this awakening.

4.8 O of what use is any discipline or practice or ritual if it does not accept all and honor all and fails to see the oneness in all?

O what of dictums or tenets that discriminate based on the skin color or cloth or style of worship or language?

O Brahman can the narrow minded highly differentiated specimens ever glimpse thee? May you allow them also the benefit of grace in a moment of compassion?

So many learned scholars profess one-sided opinions and live biased lives, so many nations enforce one law to fit all.

Never mind, the verses uttered by a Master can cleave and heal, his compassion can destroy the pockets of stubbornness. Pray someone can get initiation by an enlightened master, and the veil of ignorance is torn asunder.

4.9 O how beautiful! O what a wonder.

O how is it possible, how is it done?

A part of thee (MIND) is so confused, a part of thee (SOUL) is so clear.

A part of thee is the Lord and a part of thee is the SLAVE. Is that the way to produce merriment? Is that a common law for entertainment?

Perhaps contrast gives rise to pleasure, perhaps the up after a down is really something.

Time and again the scriptures say - if you wish to unite in yoga, then have a discipline of havan, satsang and celibacy.

Have a control over sleep, food, and entertainment. And paths will open for you to walk free, paths will open and lead you to bliss.

And what of those who are wayward and lethargic. Well they keep spinning endlessly like tops, tightly bound, almost imprisoned.

4.10 Ok, so it means both the true and the false coexist in creation.

Truth is that which stands firm under trying circumstances, falsehood crumbles when faced with inquisition.

The great Lord allows both, and all combinations of principles as well. It is up to you to choose your inclination, and then follow your gut feeling to the end. Whenever in doubt, know that Truth triumphs, albeit in the end.

This is where discipline comes in. Discipline ensures you do not give up or give in, it helps keep you on track, and it makes the difficult times pass by without scar.

4.11 Understand it well. The good Lord manifests infinity in the physical and practical domain.

What does this mean? Does it mean that the same Lord who is glorified as the best and strongest and swiftest, also shows up as the middling or the worse, the weak or the hypocrite, the lame or the lethargic?

Be very careful. Now stop and remove all bias and notion.

The same Lord who is prayed to by all and who is the support and fountain of bliss, also reflects as this mundane creation with all its bile and humor. The physical beings and human gadgets and endeavors and manmade laws, all derive their identity, their current, their half-life and their impact from the same strand of pure divinity. The emotional turbulences and the terrible storms are all powered by the one source.

Does that mean that God is mean or temperamental or stupid. Not at all. Do not go on this track, since it shall only lead to your own downfall and pain.

Then how to use or interpret the Lord's infinite nature? It must be awakened and assimilated within oneself that even though right is right and wrong is wrong, still one cannot do wrong against wrong.

The teaching is given to prevent the seed of hatred, bitterness, non-forgiveness, rigidity, or guile from taking root. When an ignorant man commits a blunder, to save one's inherent innocence, one must attribute the incident to the mysterious ways of the Lord, rather than attaching blame on a person, gadget, institution or nation.

The one who can see beyond a localized event, sees the

great lord's affable smile, and is freed from limiting prejudice, is freed from karmic impressions, and is able to perform to optimum potential and live a really cool life.

4.12 O almighty! May we hark to thy teaching and heed thy word. May our bias and notion be fluid and our memory be clear.

May we walk calmly, courageously, and with ample faith.

4.13 May we sing thy glory, may we relate heroic stories to grandchildren.

May we take out time to welcome the physical God FIRE, by lighting lamps, doing havan along with cheering, clapping and singing.

4.14 O heaven! May we strive to see the sliver of grace in the gloomy cloud, may we acknowledge thy hand in our failure and so do inner contemplation.

May we see the pro in every con, may we enhance our skill and broaden our vision to lend a helping hand.

4.15 O Brahman! May we understand the contradiction that even though all are thee, yet thee never are where wickedness brews.

Thee are not at all aware of the cruel demonic currents that surface once in a while, since thee are far far away. Thee are fast asleep and curled up in a furry ball, oblivious to the tyrannical events unfolding.

Thee manifest in your effulgent ignorance annihilating light only in particular modes of time space combinations. You remain unperturbed, hidden it is said, till the very last.

Hence the sages introduce the concept of Vastu to welcome thee while constructing homes and temples, and honor the Shivaratri and Navaratri as being times of your abundant availability.

4.16 You arise within minds at will, you visit when one is totally unsuspecting, your prick to the conscience is felt only by the soft heart.

Hence we say that guests are gods, hence we say that strangers can be saviors.

4.17 Only a gentle heart can accommodate your generous frame, a tight mind is unable to let you in.

You rub like sandpaper against the blunt and sharp emotions, you tear down narrow intellects and bulldoze crowded neural streets, such men shudder to give you passage.

The Upanishads call you as - not this, not that, not anything else either, so that men may not cage you or idolize only a particular form of yours.

The Upanishads describe you as everything, as nothing, as neither of the two, as both simultaneously, and also as that which the intellect cannot reason out, nor the senses can grasp.

Please may we not hang on to picture frames or banana skins, may we not make assumptions regarding a coconut without ever opening it and looking in.

4.18 May we understand that weekdays and weekends are societal constructs, may we understand that religions and cultures are time space dependent.

May we not label day as good or night as bad, may we not fall prey to notions of my family alone is royal or needy.

May we not enforce laws without listening to the presence, may we not go on mob fury due to misguided elders.

May the early Sunlight be our rudder, may the wisdom of Sages be our raft.

4.19 Please may we not think we alone have realized Him, may we not strut about in enlightenment.

No idols, nay no definition of God can light a candle unto Him.

He that is Great is gigantic and unknown, fine and invisible.

4.20 We make many pictures and idols and yantras of Him, we worship Him by different names and forms and rituals.

Each belief and each method is sufficient to reach Him, though none can be said to be exclusive.

Each path and all names lead to Him, never for a moment

claim your path is superior.

4.21 Seasons are sinusoidal, Nature is cyclic, history repeats itself.

How may we say 'this is the start and that is the end'?

Whichever time and season is now, may we welcome thee forthwith without losing the opportunity.

May we make you the priority, may we run to join the kindness wagon, sing lustily, and dance to our heart's content.

4.22 O Divine Lord Rudra! May we enjoy the togetherness of Rudra abhisheka. May our children and grandchildren and neighbors not miss this rare bounty.

May we not be stuck in other activity in our mind during Abhisheka. If we cannot help the proceedings or be in awe of the spectacle, may we simply close our eyes and be lost in meditation.

O Rudra! It is a great fortune to partake of your divine glory in puja, to organize a puja, or to simply invite near and dear ones to the puja.

5th Teaching (living the Brahman)

Transactional aspect of Brahman

5.1 Brahman is said to be dual. The infinite when it starts to transact, divides itself in small finite pieces so that a dialog and a play can be enacted.

In this movie, the protagonist and the antagonist both get prominent roles. The hidden heroine is the prize, both vie for her, forgetting that the real hero is within.

Brahman watches the play nonplussed. We cannot say that he takes either side. The hero goes on to prove himself worthy, the villain chooses to make himself detested.

5.2 When prayers happen, when there is non-feverish worship, He takes birth as happy and strong children, or as blooming flowers and luscious fruit, or even as diamond and mineral ore.

He becomes the elements of the periodic table and the disciplines of university study, and also the inventions and discoveries.

5.3 One set of laws is made to usher in the Satyug, another set proves to be Kalyug.

Even though spaced out in time, the laws get superseded by the earnest devotees, and for them the laws yield with glee.

Some say the laws are permanent, others acknowledge their impermanence. Both however agree on the supremacy of Brahman, both seek Him alone.

5.4 All homes are lit by the morning sunlight, all fires glow by the same principle.

All smiles arouse and excite, all fruits wish to be plucked.

The credit goes to Him, He chooses to become the exciter, the nourisher, and the Attraction.

5.5 He doesn't lift a finger, His presence alone causes all flutter and hustle and bustle.

He doesn't will anything, yet all laws seek his approval and praise. Gravity, electricity, love and excitement, all hope to please Him.

The three states of matter, the three divisions of time, the three components of every atom, grandfather father and son, all function by His grace, all sway to His wave.

5.6 And what is this esoteric teaching that is available to the earnest and sincere? That gets revealed within by yogic discipline?

That is not understood by temple preaching or hasty ritual? That can take more than a lifetime of persistent enquiry?

The Upanishad says, first open your door wide, remove bias, clean your memory. Be available to accept a living Master in the present. Do not close the door of the intellect based on past principle. Do not live 500 years in historical context. Your mind is new, your clothes are new, your tongue is new and your wife is new.

Sit in Satsang, absorb the Master's words through each pore. Maintain discipline in eating and entertainment. Slowly the haze over Brahman thins, the mist clears and the Lord is experienced.

5.7 Brahman dispenses the fruits to the sincere seeker, who is living in balance and intensely longing for bliss.

Brahman designs situations and creates platforms for individuals according to their capacity and inclination.

Brahman moves softly and silently unknown and unnoticed. He rejoices with the happy, and ignores those too entangled.

His mighty triad of Sattva Rajas Tamas creates innumerable phenomena to keep all beings and all things fully occupied.

Even though most beings and things ultimately dissolve in the Lord, the ones who follow an equation of 40% sattva 40% rajas and 20% tamas cross the finishing line quicker.

And what are the three aims each particle of matter and each wavelet of energy strives for?
Having good company, (Love)
Being able to express freely, (Acceptance)
Shining in at least one virtue. (Pride)

5.8 Thumb is the easiest example that comes to mind when we need to express the inexpressible.

We all have a thumb and know it is indispensable in day-to-day work. We express self-identity by showing the thumb.

The toy soldiers, cars and animals that children play with, are made thumb size too.

The Upanishad says that the soul inside us is thumb size. Its throne is placed in the region of the heart, or the center of the chest, and this is said just for conveying the idea that the soul is the boss and is centrally located.

Further it is stated that the soul shines brilliantly, to mean that it is pure divinity, and also to mean that each particle of creation is infused with Brahman.

Now what does a soul within a body Lord over? Naturally the soul shall play the part suited to its body. Just as in a fancy dress competition, the child who becomes a milkmaid acts like her, the one who becomes a tiger roars and growls, the one who becomes a motorcycle zooms past.

Similarly, seeing its body, the soul acts accordingly. If it is a flute, it plays soothing notes, if it is a scorpion it bites, if it is a saint it heals, and if it is salt it makes food tasty.

Here one additional point is to be understood. In the body of anything else except man, the traits of the body are well known and largely without exception. However in the body of man, it is so decreed that one may play any role. Man's nervous system has been so designed that it can express infinity, or it can express any particle or idea of creation.

Thus we learn that buddhi or reason may accept the body and perform accordingly, or it may very well set out to do the unthinkable and the incredible.

A cobbler's awl is mentioned to indicate that the soul takes

a body - by means of a sperm that is shaped like an awl,
- the soul like an awl can drill holes and guide the stitch, i.e.
it can guide the reason to take proper decisions. It also
means that blocked intellects simply need a bit of piercing
just as ear piercing transforms the personality
- proper shoes should be a high priority item and must be
carefully chosen to suit one's personality and role, apart
from being comfortable and functional.
- the shoe is a symbol of movement or evolution of soul.

5.9 Now to remove any notion of size or color or shape that
the student may visualize as being the soul, it is stated that
the actual size of the soul is finer than a hair split ten
thousand times.

I.e. the pure divinity within man is practically invisible, and
we should not give it any color or shape that our senses can
grasp. Hence a particular form or idol of God is not the only
one, any other ideology giving another form must be equally
acceptable.

The Upanishad goes on to say that the pure divine soul is
always aiming to merge into the infinite purity, i.e. like a
sunray it has the potential to withdraw backwards into the
sun.

5.10 The soul is not tied to a woman's body at all times,
the soul is also reborn as a man.

The soul is not confined to humans alone, it manifests in
every gadget, thing, herb, medicine, home, religion,
principle, flower or photon as well.

5.11 The embodied soul evolves into a new body or a
higher plane with each successive birth.

It directs the intellect at times, at other times when it has
gone out of the body, the intellect runs on auto pilot, and is
much prone to error. The soul thus enjoys a managed and
an unmanaged tenure, since by nature it is neither tied to
the body, nor does a particular body fascinate it more.

The rare Master understands this inherently, and rarely does
the soul take a Masterly body.

In other words there are innumerable body choices in the
non-living and living spectrum, and the soul doesn't
particularly favor any.

The Brahman is present in various bodies as individual
souls. Each soul has differing levels of brightness or
amplitude. Like a stream has tributaries, like the electric
supply has different wattages in each household.

5.12 Whether gross or subtle, rich or poor, handsome or
ugly, each name and form has many traits that justify its
appearance, and some traits that bewilder and cause a
wonder.

The soul is able to transform even a coward to a hero of
famous exploits, when its body is blessed by the glance of a
Master, and when it starts to implement the will of the
Master.

The Master is simply a brighter soul, and it can make the
dimmest soul qualify for the ultimate.

A current may be weak, and the light may be dull, a body might be mighty and have many powers to support it, but if the Master is missing (like the absence of a soccer coach or a secretary to the minister), then the evolution takes a downward spiral.

Even for such suffering, discarded or wrongly guided souls, the end is the same, dissolution in Brahman.

5.13 Can you say who came first, can you pinpoint where time starts and where space ends?

Such unanswered questions are faced by us regularly. We also do not know what our son wants or who our daughter is planning to marry. Nor can we foresee who shall win the election, or who shall be the next genius.

In spite of uncertainty, there is a strong faith 'i am well taken care of'. In spite of chaos, there is a striking beauty in nature. In spite of traffic snarls and long driving times, there is a hope 'i shall make it'.

Who or what is this faith? What is hope? Even the newborn birds, saplings, and little puppies know that they will be looked after. Their needs shall be met. Their desires and longings shall be quenched.

What is there in creation that gives such a guarantee? Who is He that takes the responsibility of events that none can bear? Who ensures that planes and rockets shall land safely? Who fills a mother with love for her newborn?

Do you ever ponder? Do you ever seek? The wise say - the

man who embarks on the search for Lord is the one who is the most fortunate.

5.14 He is known as Shiva. The auspicious. Ś i v a. Ś for *shanti* = calmness. i for *iti* = right now and here. v for *vishwas* = deep faith. a for *aang* = all inclusive and all pervasive.

And how to know Him? Through the grace of the Master. Through a light that is stronger and can illuminate Him.

In the inner recesses of the heart which feels a moment of freedom and love. In the corner of the mind that has a moment of silent contemplation.

And by what name to call Him? Devi Durga Radha Ganesha Krishna Nanak Mahavir? Or any other? The Upanishad says 'He answers to all names'. He knows He is being called irrespective of your station or nationality. Irrespective of your language or style of calling.

And how do we know He has heard? Only the heart shall know. His appearance and form cannot be drawn, His manner and personality cannot be stated. But whosoever glimpses Him shall know. His nectar shall remain. His bliss shall light your way.

6th Teaching (leela of Brahman)

The cosmic play of Brahman

6.1

The pundits and scholars and academics are divided over the origin and cause of the universe. A large number believe there is independent control of many things and principles, i.e. there are many independent forces that govern the creation.

Then some others are of the view that there is a ruler of time, and that in turn gives life to all particles.

Both have a point, and there is certainly someone Other as well that governs it all. The great Lord whom none can define, yet all can intuitively feel.

The Lord's wheel all experience as a set of ups and downs, as birth and death, as beginning and finishing, as irritating pin pricks or small victories, as waves of doubt or of all is well.

6.2

The Lord's mystery is deepened due to the fact that he is at times, and then he is not within the folds of creation. At one moment He is in the smile of a child, and the next moment He's gone. He is present in some graceful activity, but He never stays for long.

Like the intense passion, the awe of wonder, the deep longing, the final burst to cross the finishing line, all earth-shaking in magnitude but encapsulated in a momentary flash.

The Lord has given each immense free will. There is a large degree of latitude and lots of options, many paths. He is not going to fix anyone's will, nor does He bother to prevent anyone from blunder. He plays a game of "do what you want, it shall affect you alone, for me all is acceptable".

Very hard to digest, impossible to reason out are His ways. At the end of each one's allotted timespan, (400 years for human beings), all merge into Him, all achieve union with Him.

Whether Time, whether Nature, whether an atom of Space, the Lord is present therein, however none of them is the Lord. The Lord prefers to be dormant. Even though present, as if He is not.

It cannot be said He caused an event, yet it is hard to dissociate Him from anything.

He is certainly not the cruel tyrant who is causing hell all around. He is certainly not the stupid moron who is responsible for wastage of natural resources or who causes pollution and emotional upheavel.

Yet can we say He doesn't notice these things? Can we say the ignorant do not derive ignorance by His will?

Some questions cannot so simply be answered. All that can be said is the Lord causes no harm, nor any destruction or any turmoil. The Lord does not stand in the way of anyone's success. The Lord does not cause illness or poverty.

Then does earth make mistakes? Does water choose to become polluted? Does fire cause wilful damage? Does air become unbreathable? And does space run out?

6.3

The answer to the above is rather hazy. One explanation given is that man reaps the fruit of his own sowing. Some men due to bitterness sow terrible seeds that sprout to cause suffering. The Upanishad says the suffering cannot touch the pure. The innocent can never fall prey to wickedness.

Sometimes it may appear that a good man is being abused, however deep inside there are wounds and errors yet unrepented for and brushed aside, so the memory has forgotten its own earlier terrible actions.

The union with the divine is everyone's longing, however when one's actions and attitude do not qualify for the same, then it is impossible that He shall manifest in one's life.

Brahman gives chances, or creates situations for man to evolve. It is noticed that the brave make the grade in the first attempt itself. They are the ones who are hailed as the enlightened masters. For them" soham that is me", this one principle manifests.

The ones with intense passion are next to cross over, and a close third are those who do not give up.

Passion is Bhakti and the second principle after bravery.

Doggedness or purusharth is the third principle that manifests at the middle of the pyramid.

Then we see the devotees and disciples who heed the words of the master and are willing to make a u-turn in life. These ordinary men and women are unnoticed by the media, are present in every town, and make use of one facet of Yoga.

In them, one of the eight cornerstones of Yoga is blossomed. It could be Ahimsa or compassion, it could be asana or body

fitness,
It could be pranayama or control of emotions, it could be pratyahara or control of senses, dharana one-pointedness in speech and action, dhyana contemplation on who am i and what is my purpose, or samadhi letting go in total surrender.

6.4

In the beginning a child or a disciple is open and accepting, with regard and belongingness for all. Thereafter a particular discipline and master and mode of living takes prominence and undue distractions and time and energy leakages get limited.

This helps preserve the vitality so needed for the smooth journey of a 400-year lifespan, and it also minimizes the moments when one is out of tune with nature.

A day comes when fear and suffering bid final adieu, and nature envelops the devotee in an impregnable force field where fountains of bliss and uninhibited adventures spring.

6.5

Such a devotee glimpses the great Lord, and his gratefulness knows no bounds.

The devotee acknowledges a supreme oneness in creation where a beginning is an ending, where all endings are new beginnings, where cause and effect are strongly intertwined, and each effect is a new cause.

He sees each man as someone's savior, behelds each woman with a beloved, his journey then becomes timeless, ageless, tireless. Time answers to his needs, Time dilates to accomodate his pace, Time ensures his timeliness.

Such a devotee is adored by generations, such a devotee becomes a legend. What he does sets a precedence, what he wishes becomes the wish of the populace.

6.6
Such a devotee is protected by trees, acknowledged by phenomena, and shaped by the unknown.

Such a devotee can mix elements and create wonders at will. He can shape the destiny of individuals as well as of nations. He can banish suffering and join broken hearts. He can cause euphoria in families and cities.

We all hope to perceive the brilliant Lord in this small frame, quiet tongue and nondescript appearance.

6.7
The rare one who acknowledges such a devotee, who honors him completely, who sees in him the source, that rare soul transcends the cloud web and crosses over the sea of unending travail.

We are fortunate to be such rare seekers, we are the blessed ones who glimpsed the Lord and touched infinity.

By some unknown coincidence, we saw through the veil. We saw a bar of solid gold-like glow of divinity, a beam of purity and in a flash our intellect bowed with full support of the ego. Our consciousness made way for the big, for the superior, for the vast. Our soul welcomed whole-heartedly the brilliant light, the splendorous magnificence.

6.8

Not just for a rare devotee, nor just to unusual seeking, the Lord answers to calls which cannot be adequately described, which cannot be logically deduced, which have never been mentioned nor written.

The Lord's workmanship and His class are so well hidden that none except the brave ever attempts or grasps. The Lord's plan and strategy are coded deep into each nucleus, His design blueprint is woven tightly in every fold of space and every instance of time.

Matter transforms to life, energy condenses to matter, thoughts dream and emotions cleave, His signature is not evident to the smartest, His workmanship goes unperceived by the city folk.

The masterly unknown is unremembered while the local lads and supermoms get all the credit. Those who try to talk of Him limit Him severely by their narrow bias, the pundits prattle of Him in metaphors that do not do Him justice.

O who can describe the Undescribable, who can portray Him who creates the sun and the blackhole?

6.9

Brahman has the uniqueness of being a husband to both the men and the women. And also to the non-living. Husband here meaning the provider, the taking care, the security, and the guarantee.

Brahman is the entity that causes rulers to function, that makes it appear to the president that he is in charge, that instills a notion in the emperor that his dominion is his.

Brahman doesn't have a fixed shape or form or any characteristic that is clearly identifiable. Brahman is impervious to the senses and beyond any logical or illogical reasoning. Brahman manifests at will in things big or small, beautiful or weird.

Brahman can tune to any wavelength, Brahman can be friends with any temperament.

Brahman is beyond cause and effect. Brahman is the parent and the sibling, the child and the distant relative. Brahman is the ruler and the ruled, Brahman is beyond rules.

6.10

An allegory is painted. A spider and its web is told.

Man uses brick and cement and stuff other than his body and not born of his body to fashion dwellings. He furnishes himself with comforts not produced of his genes.

Brahman doesn't need a dwelling, Brahman is not interested in any production, yet this universe is as if made by Him to suit His taste. The currents and energies are like luminous strands, the forces of nature are like a criss-cross web.

O compassionate Brahman! May thee resolve our conflicts and banish our doubts. May thee just in a trice accept us in thy embrace.

6.11

O such wonder! Thee are in us and beside us and ever ready
to lend a hand, but our radar cannot identify thy presence
and our intellect cannot digest thy variability.

Even most of our involuntary functions are guided and
made operational by thee alone.

All our pragmatic efforts bear fruits by thy grace alone. Our
healthy emotions are a direct result of your compassion. Our
able works and sound judgements stem only due to your
attendance.

We hope you preside over our errors and commissions too,
though it is clear you are not aware of such occurrences at
all. You are no witness to crime and negligence, you are no
accomplice to pride and prejudice.

Our headaches and heartburns, our lust and infatuation are
far far far removed from thy will, thy sight, and thy
involvement.

6.12

Strolling along alone on the timeSpace motorway, Brahman
suddenly boomed, without a thought.

At that time thought currents were absent. In a flash varied
thoughts manifested and innumerable things and beings
and energies took birth.

It is said one in ten million get to glimpse the Brahman who
is behind and below, within, and above and in front of it all.

This glimpse is a nectar like force that over time ensures freedom by guiding the path, correcting the imbalances, and charting a course of self-discipline or Yoga.

Freedom from what? From the notion "i am this body and these are my assets and this is my status and purpose", and likewise all other types of (un)limited fancies.

6.13

Have you ever thought, "who or what propels me, inspires me, causes likes and dislikes in me, frustrations or excitements, infuses my vision and mission?"

The Upanishad says there is an imperceptible entity flowing within and pervading the entire space. This entity known as Brahman is not graspable by any means, neither is it certain which thought and what act is Its will.

In most cases, one may directly attribute noble, sacred, benevolent and extraordinary acts to His will. In some cases, harsh and unpleasant acts are also His will, when seen in the context of a larger timeSpace band, while "some good" acts are certainly not His will when seen accordingly.

A fundamental aspect of creation, known as the mathematical principle, and all of the math that governs creation, known as Sankhya or balanced design, is a direct evidence of Brahman or a superior entity that none controls or can interface with, yet that oversees all and remains unaffected and unaltered across eons.

The subtle aspect of creation known as Yoga, which comes into play in human beings and higher beings like bhakta, siddha, gandharva, yaksa, apsara, also aims for Brahman.

Yoga and Yogic teachings highlight the universal force and unity inherent in creation, and strive to make man rise above his limited frame or touchy identity and touch infinity.

6.14

Brahman's aspect is supposed to be far more than the transactable universe.

Apart from blackholes, star clusters, nebulae, quasars; or the principles of gravity, magnetism, acceleration; or fundamental particles like photons and phonons; or the deep emotions of romantic love, Brahman has aspects that are new and newly discovered, that keep getting known bit by bit, and technologies and gadgets that can forever be tweaked and improved upon and invented.

With each successive slice of history, previously unheard of phenomena come to light, some principles become extinct, new ones get created.

Brahman is not limited by men or machines or nature, Brahman is not bound by principles nor by fundamental particles.

No being whether saint or king or scientist or genius or deity can ever gauge the possibilities of Brahman, no principle can ever circumambulate Him.

Brahman is the oil that keeps joints functional, flames lit, and love available. Brahman is the glue that helps join minds, Brahman is the power that powers electric currents,

Brahman is the compassion in an innocent heart.

6.15

An allegory is portrayed here. Some characteristics of the bird known as Swan are highlighted as desirable and ideal, pure whiteness, herbivorous, mating for life, protective of family, symbol of glowing light and soothing sound, feathers that remain absolutely dry even though the swan swims.

Mythology also credits a swan to be able to pick out milk molecules from a mixture of milk and water, and the ability to travel to planes where the soul alone can travel.

The unknown and undiscernable Brahman is said to have such desirable properties by depicting a known entity like swan.

A swan spends a large time in water, and gleams like a bright flame in an expanse of blue. This is the quality of Brahman, as if hot fire on a lake, atonce cooling and warming, atonce vertical and flat, atonce dancing and still.

O rare seeker! O ye who can appreciate this! O he who can think what cannot be thought, who has faith in the unknown, who treads far beyond his comfort zone, who revels in the entirety! Only thee qualifies for nirvana, only thee can respect freedom, only thee can stomach absorption in the Divine.

6.16

He who permeates the fabric of the universe and is within each molecule, can verily be said to be the emperor.

His emperorship is unique and unmatched, since what He wills it happens, what He wills doesn't happen due to His granting of free will, and what He does not will also happens.

The beauty is not that all these three possibilities exist simultaneously, but these possibilities exist based on time slices or yuga. In a certain time slice known as Satyug, His will dominates in entirety. In another time slice known as Kalyug His will exhibits all three flavors.

Again in space slices known as loka, these three possibilities coexist or exist independently.

Finally in body constructs known as yoni, these possibilities are seen to both coexist or exist independently.

Such is the masterly governance, such is the precise handling, such is His astute emperorship.

Free will can be a good thing in moderation. Indiscipline can be tolerated in certain situations. Both a genius and a dumbo can be the cause of much grief or heavenly happiness or vice versa in separate instances.

One man's meat is another man's poison, a right here is a wrong there, those wedded to each other might both enjoy cool, or might have a mix of hot and cold.

What is seen, perceived and understood from one point of reference can change its entire theory or nature from another plane.

There is no end to the magic, miracles are happening in rapid succession, truth triumphs but in the end.

6.17

His working is entirely a mystery, very deep, hard to fathom, not within the grasp of the intelligent nor the talented.

Nature doesn't ever give up nor lose patience, so do not ever tempt Her no matter how big you become.

6.18-19

All parents give birth to a son, whom they educate to their maximum capacity, then send into the world, hoping for the best.

That brilliant son, whose intellect remains transparent, whose heart remains in sync, who gets the desire for liberation, such is the son whom the parents bow down to.

This son is so simple that he displays an astonishing level of innocence, purity that is a lifetime's effort to maintain, self humbling patience, and extreme bravery.

Such a son crosses the bridge to infinity, having burnt all connections and bindings.

6.20

When a number of such sons shall discover space travel and recount adventures across the galactic plains,

When maidens shall glow and charm heavens with their spotless beauty, making them arch down to shower bliss on their lovers,

Then all those in the vicinity without much effort nor enough merit, too shall glimpse the freedom, and be ferried across due to their proximity.

6.21
One such son who was fair, one such maiden who was dark, both by their complete faith in the Divine and their total acceptance of each other,

Got the showers of love and bliss, got established in divine will.

Their words became nectar to all eager listeners, their story tore away their afflictions,

they were enshrined for ever in the hearts of men.

6.22
The knowledge shared in this Upanishad had already been revealed to men who walked long before,

It cannot be absorbed by the sullen, nor by the wicked son, or by the frivolous daughter.

It cannot be understood nor digested or made use of by any cheat.

6.23
The son whose devotion is profound, who seeks and befriends a living master,

who adores the Master like the Lord making no distinction,

To such a son these words take root, sprout, blossom and
bear fruit.

The fruit of eternity, the fruit of bliss,

Yes, this is the nectar that the great Lord grants,

Yes this is the only joy worth seeking.

Etymology of Upanishad

Consider Adi Shankaracharya's derivation of the word 'Upanishad' as given in his bhashyam on the Katha Upanishad.

upa + ni + ṣad + kvip –> upaniṣad

The Sanskrit root from Dhatupatha 1c - 854, 6c - 1427 "ṣadḷ viśaraṇa–gati–avasādaneṣu" has the three meanings,

namely viśaraṇa = wither, gati = attain, avasādana = sit close.

In the context of wisdom, we can say
  - wither away one's stupidity
  - attain liberation
  - sit with a conviction

The upasarga "upa" stands for nearness, closeness.
The upasarga "ni" stands for delving into, intense.
The pratyaya "kvip" makes a noun, and while joining, it vanishes entirely.

Thus the word 'Upanishad' is formed, and it has the meaning of destroying one's ignorance and granting freedom, when we sit devotedly at the feet of the Master.

References

https://www.ashtangayoga.info/philosophy/sanskrit-and-devanagari/transliteration-tool/#devanagari/iast

https://www.learnsanskrit.cc/
https://upanishads.org.in/

Guided Meditations Sri Sri Ravi Shankar
https://www.youtube.com/watch?v=ECHxnCJYrpM
https://www.youtube.com/watch?v=vzzWLZb4a4g

Swami Nikhilananda – The Upanishads Vol I & II – 1st – 1952 – Harper & Brothers Publishers, New York.

Harikrishnadas Goyandka – Ishadi Nau Upanishad (Hindi) – 36th Reprint - 2017 – Gita Press, Gorakhpur.

Ashwini Kumar Aggarwal
     – Ishavasya Upanishad – 1st – 2019 –
     – Kena Upanishad – 1st – 2019 –
     – Katha Upanishad – 1st – 2019 –
     – Mandukya Upanishad – 1st – 2019 –
     – Mundaka Upanishad – 1st – 2020 –
     – Prashna Upanishad – 1st – 2020 –
     – Aitareya Upanishad – 1st – 2020 –
     – Shvetashvatara Upanishad – 1st – 2021 –
Devotees of Sri Sri Ravi Shankar Ashram, Punjab.

Individual Upanishad Books Links

ISHAVASYA

KENA

KATHA

MANDUKYA

MUNDAKA

PRASHNA

AITAREYA

SHVETASHVATARA

https://advaita56.
weebly.com
/books.html

Epilogue

Time is needed. Effort is needed. The Will is paramount. Any Great Work needs something more, a liitle bit extra everyday, a shower of Grace regularly.

Do we qualify for the Grace? For sure. All of us do.
What about Vision? It needs a Guru. A Master.
And how about that extra effort Everyday?
That is all about Upbringing and Education.

सर्वे भवन्तु सुखिनः । सर्वे सन्तु निरामया ।

सर्वे भद्राणि पश्यन्तु । मा कश्चिद् दुःख भाग्भवेत् ॥

ॐ शान्तिः शान्तिः शान्तिः ॥

sarve bhavantu sukhinaḥ | sarve santu nirāmayāḥ |

sarve bhadrāṇi paśyantu | mā kaścid duḥkha bhāgbhavet ||

oṃ śānti śānti śāntiḥ ||

When faith has blossomed in life, Every step is led by the Divine.

Sri Sri Ravi Shankar

Om Namah Shivaya

जय गुरुदेव

www.ingramcontent.com/pod-product-compliance
Lightning Source LLC
Chambersburg PA
CBHW020902160726

47993CB00005B/1776